Selling Sanity

The Troubled-Teen Industry, the Insane Profits, and the Kids Who Pay the Price

Corey Jentry, Ph.D.

Truth Forward Media Group

ISBN 979-8-9997139-0-2

Contents

Introduction

I was a broken kid. Messed up. Unstable. I want you to know that right upfront. Not for any sympathy or shock value. But because it was pivotal to why I ended up where I did. I made bad decisions, but mostly I was just trying to survive something I couldn't name yet. Like a lot of kids in pain, I reached out for help, desperate for belonging, purpose, and a place where I didn't feel invisible.

I didn't get forced into treatment. I walked in. Lied to get through the door. I said what they wanted to hear because I needed something—anything—to hold onto.

What I found instead was a system built on selling sanity.

A recovery program that promised healing but demanded obedience. It used the language of love and accountability while keeping everyone locked into fear, shame, and control. It didn't care whether you got better. It cared whether you stayed in line and whether your parents kept paying.

This isn't just my story. It's part memoir, part investigation. A look inside an industry that profits from pain and markets manipulation as therapy. Its so-called "troubled-teen" system thrives by turning vulnerability into revenue and survival into silence.

I believed I was walking into help. What I walked into was a business. And like many others, I didn't come out healed. I came out more broken than when I went in.

As you read this book, you'll see me use the terms "treatment-recovery industry" and "troubled-teen industry" a lot. That's not by accident. I don't use either term lightly, and I'm not just being provocative. I use them because this particular corner of behavioral health is full of programs that, while claiming to help struggling young people, often end up doing more harm than good.

It's a sprawling and diverse industry (to be contrasted with the profession below), but with one disturbing through line: unethical, sometimes outright abusive practices disguised as treatment. Beneath it all is a steady focus on profit. When you look past the mission statements and glossy brochures, you find that far too many programs aren't really about recovery. They're about revenue.

This isn't speculation or sensationalism. Behavioral health makes up about 20% of all health care fraud in the U.S. Let that sink in. Up to $20 billion is lost to health care fraud from this sector each year.[1] That should make all of us pause and really take a hard look at how these programs operate.

One well-known example is a model developed by Bob Meehan, whose approach to recovery has influenced countless programs over the years. Meehan's philosophy, while wrapped in language about tough love and accountability, often relied on emotional manipulation, shame-based tactics, and rigid groupthink. Even though some programs may not follow his model exactly, many copy its authoritarian style, adding their own untested, unregulated methods that aren't backed by clinical research.[2]

So why do these programs keep popping up and continue to grow despite the harm they cause?

One word: oversight. Or rather, the lack of it.

There's no national system monitoring and holding these programs accountable in any meaningful way. Licensing requirements vary wildly from state to state. Many of the programs operate in gray areas where regulations are either poorly defined or loosely enforced. These all work together to let opportunistic providers operate, sometimes for years, without facing consequences.

It's often only after a serious incident makes headlines or a former client speaks up that the public learns how damaging some of these places can be. By then, the harm is already done.

But I want to be clear: not all recovery programs are harmful. Some are genuinely good, rooted in medicine, clinical evidence, and ethical care. To help make the distinction, I use two specific categories throughout this book: *industry* and *profession*.

When I say *industry,* I'm referring to programs that prioritize profit over people. These are facilities where questionable practices, punitive policies, and coercive tactics are normalized. This is where most of the abuse, neglect, and lasting damage takes place.

By contrast, the *profession* refers to the treatment centers, clinicians, mentors, and programs doing the hard work of ethical, effective care. These people and places follow best practices, use trauma-informed approaches, and respect the people they serve. In the profession, the pillars of treatment are ethics, transparency, and true commitment to healing—not control.

Keeping this distinction in mind as you move through the chapters ahead is crucial. It keeps the focus on the programs that are causing harm. It helps push reform in the right direction toward greater oversight, higher standards, and better outcomes.

One dynamic I focus on over the span of several chapters is what happens when someone gets kicked out of a program. How a program handles expulsion reveals a lot about its values and ethics.

To be fair, expelling someone might sometimes be justified. If a young person is violent or needs a higher level of care, a responsible discharge—with a proper handoff—is necessary.

But that's not what I'm talking about.

What I'm addressing is how frequently and casually expulsion is used in industry-based programs. Rather than seeing expulsion as a clinical last resort, these programs use it as a tool for control. Participants are expelled for missing a meeting, for challenging authority, or even for relapsing—something that should be viewed as a symptom of the very condition the program is supposed to treat.

These expulsions are punitive and performative. They're meant to reinforce the program's dominance, to scare others into compliance, or to get rid of someone who's become inconvenient. And what's worse is that many of these discharges are sudden, undocumented, and done with zero consideration for the person's ongoing needs.

The impact can be devastating for the person getting expelled. It reinforces shame. It breaks trust. It deepens trauma. It also sends a chilling message to the people left behind: *Step out of line, and you're next.*

Compare that to how ethical programs handle things.

They don't treat relapse or resistance as failure but as feedback. If a young person struggles to engage in treatment, they don't throw them out. They lean in. They adapt. They ask questions like: *What's not working here? What do they need that we aren't providing?*

When discharge is truly necessary, it's handled with care. It's planned and documented. The family is involved. The person isn't left to fend for themselves or dumped into a worse situation. There's a clear path forward—whether that's a different type of program, a higher level of care, or a reintegration back into their home community.

It's easy to see how programs grounded in ethics differ from those driven by fear and profit. A big worry now is how fast the treatment recovery industry is growing as so many new unethical programs open their doors, attract families in crisis, and operate without scrutiny. And it's not just due to limited oversight and patchy regulations.

These programs know how to market themselves. They know the right buzzwords. They know how to look legitimate, even when their methods aren't. And in the absence of strong regulatory frameworks, they continue to attract funding, fill beds, and bill insurance companies—often while doing real, lasting harm to the people they claim to help.

We have to course-correct, and we have to do it now. If we keep putting the industry first instead of the people who actually do the work, we risk letting a recovery model built on fear, control, and compliance become the norm—while healing, growth, and dignity get left behind.

What's really needed is a change in values. We have to fund programs that actually care, train professionals who do the same, and call out those who don't. We need real oversight, transparency, and honest conversations—loud enough for everyone to hear—about what good treatment should look like.

It starts with awareness, with sharing and listening to the stories that are often almost too hard to hear. We need to ask challenging questions and refuse to settle for easy answers.

So as you start to read the chapters ahead, remember this: the difference between *industry* and *profession* isn't just a word choice. It's the line between harm and healing. And for those of us who've lived through these systems, that line means everything.

Before you start chapter 1, I want to explain how I've approached sharing my personal story in this book.

The experiences I share are deeply personal—not just for me but for many others who were part of those times in my life. Some were peers. Some were staff. Some were friends or people I barely knew but haven't forgotten. To write honestly while still respecting the privacy and dignity of those individuals, I've made a few important decisions about how the story is presented.

First, some names and details have been changed to protect people's anonymity and avoid re-traumatizing anyone who didn't consent to being part of this narrative. My intention isn't to single anyone out, but to expose the systems and structures that allowed harm to take place.

Second, I've sometimes used composite characters. These figures are drawn from multiple real people whose stories shared similar patterns or dynamics. This allows me to highlight recurring themes and behaviors I witnessed without compromising anyone's privacy. It also makes room for a broader truth that doesn't belong to just one person, but speaks to a collective experience.

Lastly, I've adjusted timelines, compressing or reordering events to make the storytelling clearer and easier to follow. Real-life recovery isn't tidy. It's nonlinear, chaotic, and often hard to explain. These adjustments help bring clarity to moments that, in real time, were anything but.

I share all this because I believe telling stories—especially the hard ones—requires both honesty and care. When people's lives and pain are part of the narrative, protecting their humanity matters as much as exposing the truth.

At the end of the day, this is my story, but it's not mine alone. It echoes the experiences of many others, and I hope their voices, too, will be part of a collective story that refuses to be ignored.

ONE

I'm so freaking skinny. The thought hits me like a slap as I glance down at my forearm. Then it turns whiny. *It's hot today. I hate sweating.* Another shift. Now into frustration. *I'm such a royal fuck-up.*

That voice in my head is always screaming for attention. Loud, jagged, rowdy. It never shuts up.

My steps feel off like my thoughts. Quick and uncertain, each one trying to dodge the noise in my head. I heard someone on TV say that 13 is "such an awkward age," like it's something contagious. Some kind of goddamn plague. Yeah, no shit.

I keep my eyes on the ground as I head toward the portable classroom. It's a habit. Eyes down means no one notices you. At least that's what I tell myself. The shaky wooden steps leading to the white trailer are just ahead.

I pick up the pace when, out of nowhere—snap!—my chest jerks forward. My head whips back. My feet lift off the ground. It's all slow motion and split-second quick at the same time. Then my whole body smacks the ground.

"Trailer trash."

DeShawn. I'd know his sneer anywhere.

He leans in, pressing his full weight into my back. His hot, sour breath spills over my face as he whispers those two words again. This time, tighter and meaner.

They slice deeper than the dirt grinding into my cheek. My eyes burn with tears. My whole body aches, but his words hurt worse.

His hand grabs the back of my head, shoving my face into the gravel. His knee digs into my spine. Pressure builds. Now, the physical pain overtakes my self-contempt.

I hear laughing. Shouting. Voices urging him on.

DeShawn yanks my skinny arms behind me. I can't breathe. I'm held bound and captive by his rage.

Rage is strange. It's anger gone wild, unleashed and primal. Rage makes people lash out and lose control. I wish I could feel that kind of raw power, even for a second. But I don't. There's nothing. At all.

Warm spit lands on my neck with expert precision. Then DeShawn's final move. One more jab of his knee into my back. And, just like that, he's gone.

I stay on the ground for a few seconds. I wait until I know it's safe to move.

Finally, I push myself up, gather my books, and climb the stairs to the classroom.

I hate myself. I'm so fucking weak. My body's bruised and scraped. My face stings, dotted with red marks from the loose gravel. But worse than the pain is the spinning confusion and self-loathing I feel inside.

I slam the flimsy door of the double-wide trailer behind me. Home. And I'm alone like usual, but not really. My dad's off doing things I'm not supposed to know about (but I do), or hanging out with my little brother. My mom's in her room, door shut, curled up with her pills and booze. It's where she spends days on end, riding out the effects of her self-medicated life. She only comes out to grab a cup of coffee and then goes right back in her room.

"What the hell, Corey? Stop slamming the damn door." Her voice is hoarse and slurred.

She stumbles out of her room, bent over and holding her stomach. Her stringy hair's a mess, and her clothes look like she pulled them off the floor, which she probably did. I turn my face away, but not fast enough.

"Damn, boy. You get beat up again?"

I don't say anything.

"Turn around. Let me see."

There's no concern in her voice. She just wants to look. That used to hurt. Now, it just feels empty.

"I can already hear your father when he sees your face," she mutters.

And I could hear him, too.

"All his hollering's gonna wake me up. I already feel like shit. I wish you'd think about me for once. Quit making him mad. I need some peace and quiet around here. If you weren't always messing up, he might actually be here more and taking care of me. No one around here ever gives a damn about me."

At that moment, I wish I could have been more like De-Shawn. I wish I could have felt some rage, or at least some anger, pulsing through my body, felt some strength building up in my wiry frame. I had never been able to stand up for myself in the face of her weak but caustic words. All I felt was how my insides were twisting in knots, how her words were igniting an all-too-familiar fear in my mind that played out the same way each time—*I'm a superlative fuck-up for such a scrawny kid.*

She was right about one thing. My dad lost it when he saw my face.

He always did. I was always quick to cry and too emotional for him. He told me I embarrassed him. Said I should be more like my little brother. He was the golden boy, the baseball star. Dad always doted on him. But with me, it felt like he had tossed me to the side of the road in almost every way years ago and never looked back.

Thirteen is a weird age. That was the year my hormones kicked in, and I started noticing girls in a whole new way. But instead of feeling excited or hopeful, it made me hate myself more. I knew I didn't stand a chance with any of them. I was lanky and awkward, always growing faster than my jeans could keep up with. My voice cracked all over the place, like it couldn't decide who I was supposed to be.

Life felt like it was closing in. Like I was tied up, blindfolded, and stuck like the woman on the Eight of Swords card. Between the crap at home, the bullying at school, and everything I thought about myself, I felt trapped. I didn't know how to fix anything. I was desperate to just survive.

And then, just like that, everything changed.

"In there?" I stop walking and stare at the faded, broken-down single-wide trailer tucked away in the back corner of the neighboring trailer park. Calling me nervous doesn't even come close.

Daryl just keeps walking. "Come on, Corey."

I met Daryl a few months ago in a way you don't forget. It was after one of those beatdowns from DeShawn at school. I was starting to pick my books up off the ground when Daryl walked over, scooped them up, dusted them off, and handed them to me. He didn't say anything at all. He just gave me this small nod and a half-smile, like he knew exactly how it felt. Then he turned and walked away.

He was a couple years older, known for drinking and smoking and hanging with a rougher crowd. Maybe he was high that day, maybe not. But he helped me. And that stuck with me.

Since then, he's just kind of hovered around. Not close, not far. But always around.

I push down my fear and fall in step beside him. At the trailer door, he knocks. The flimsy metal rattles a bit before creaking open. All I see is darkness. All I smell is some funky smoke. Daryl steps in like he owns the place. I follow behind him.

"Hey, man. This is Corey. He's cool."

My eyes adjust, and I make out two guys. One is tall and skinny with messy dark hair. His name is John. The other is short and round with a buzz cut. His name is Lenny. He's sunk into the ratty couch and taking a hit from the bong in his hand.

They both look like they're in their twenties. John nods at the floor, so we sit down. He fires up another bong and starts passing it around. I watch him breathe in, hold it, then blow out this slow stream of smoke, kind of like he's showing off. He smiles at me.

Then Daryl takes a turn. He's casual and practiced. As he lets out the smoke from his mouth, he passes the bong to me.

I don't want to mess this up. I copy exactly what they did. I hold the bong right, seal my lips, and breathe in. The smoke hits hard and my chest burns. I want to cough so bad but I don't. I hold it, then let it out slow, like I know what I'm doing. I look up. They're all watching. Daryl gives me a grin. The other guys nod as I hand the bong back to John.

And then I feel it.

Not just the floaty, warm high, but something deeper. Sitting on that crappy carpet, surrounded by all the smoke and dumb jokes, I feel like I've been let in. For the first time in a long time, I don't feel like a fuck-up. I feel accepted.

Fast forward two years.

I'm in high school now. Puberty is mostly behind me. And yeah, I made it through, mostly because of Daryl. Those years were still tough. My parents didn't suddenly start caring, but weed and alcohol showed up when they didn't. They filled in the empty spots. They dulled the sting.

Daryl, though? He didn't just keep coasting. He spiraled. Always drunk, always in trouble. His life crashed and burned. He became the guy they warned you about in school assemblies.

And then, one day, he disappeared.

He actually got clean. Went to some rehab place two states away. One day he told me about it. Now, he was back and part of some other rehab program for teens. He said the kids there were actually decent. Fun. Then he grinned and said, "The girls in the group are hot. Like, seriously hot. And down."

I was a 16-year-old virgin who smoked on weekends and drank when I could. But after hearing about these people, I had to get in. I had to be part of *that* group.

TWO

Author's note: As discussed in the Introduction, I'm drawing a distinction between the profession of recovery and the industry of recovery throughout the book. When I write about the industry, I'm referring to those treatment centers and programs that practice unethical, coercive, and abusive tactics to get patients and participants as well as to manipulate and control them.

Life asks us to be vulnerable. There's just no getting around it. But most of us have the wrong idea about what that actually means. We mix it up with weakness, like being real or open somehow makes us fragile or broken. So instead of learning how to be genuinely vulnerable, we either fight the feelings that scare us or run from them completely.

But here's the thing: when we shut vulnerability down, it just messes us up. It leaves marks. On the flip side, when we actually let ourselves be seen—and when others receive that with care—it's powerful. It makes us feel human. It makes us feel *real*. Denying that part of ourselves? That's what breaks us. And if we don't deal with that pain, we end up passing it on, whether we mean to or not.

Vulnerability just wasn't a thing in my family. We didn't do it. DeShawn didn't do it. Nobody I grew up around knew how to sit with what they were feeling—especially not if it looked like weakness. It scared the hell out of them. My parents were always running—from each other, from me, from themselves. Watching them, I learned real quick that being open or honest about what hurt wasn't safe. Vulnerability wasn't something human—it was something dangerous.

And then there was DeShawn. He didn't run like my parents did. He fought. The second anything got too real, he came out swinging. That fear he carried—it was deep. And yeah, it showed up in me, too. But mine didn't come out as fight or flight. It just froze me. Locked me in place. I got stuck somewhere in the middle, with the pain building up and nowhere for it to go.

The people in my life basically taught me that I *was* weakness. My parents didn't move toward me with love when I needed it—they turned away. That kind of rejection lays the groundwork early: I started seeing myself as unlovable. And then there were people like DeShawn, who seemed to think the parts of me I hated most needed to be beaten out of me—or erased entirely. Neither reaction helped. Neither taught me anything about how to actually be vulnerable in a healthy way. All they did was reinforce the idea that vulnerability is something dangerous or shameful. And when that belief takes hold, it doesn't just hurt—it wrecks you. It sets you up for a life of self-hate, shame, and feeling broken.

The truth is, we can't learn how to do vulnerability alone. We need people who get it—people who stay with us so that we can figure out what real vulnerability actually is. Breaking out of the old patterns means unlearning all the ways we try to guard ourselves that only end up making things worse. We've got to stop letting fear run the show. Stop attacking the people around us who seem "too soft" or "too emotional." And, just as importantly, stop turning on ourselves for feeling the things we feel. That fear gets unleashed when someone dares to be open or real. It plays out in endless battles on endless fronts. And it's leaving way too many of us feeling wrecked and alone, like wartime casualties.

The troubled-teen treatment industry is a willing mercenary in these battles. It sells out its ethics and seeks to fan the flames of fear that live within broken people as they struggle to be okay, or to cope with their vulnerability. The industry has figured out that it can make insane amounts of money from broken kids who come from broken parents and broken families. It's the perfect setup for exploitation. Everyone's scared, everyone's looking for answers, and the industry shows up like a savior with promises of structure and solutions. But what they're really selling is a way to avoid the hard stuff. A way to dodge vulnerability instead of learning how to live with it.

My kind of pain was the kind that comes from deep-down brokenness. And if there was ever someone perfectly set up to be taken advantage of by the troubled-teen industry, it was me. They were selling sanity. And I was ready to buy it over and over again, whatever it took. I was drowning in isolation, shame, self-hate—you name it. It all just built up inside me until it felt like a storm I couldn't escape. I would've done anything to feel connected, to shut off the constant self-judgment in my head, to make the pain stop. And for me, that "anything" turned out to be drinking and smoking weed. I wasn't addicted, not really, but it helped me get through middle school. It numbed things just enough so I could survive the day. At the time, it felt like it worked. But looking back, I can see it was just a temporary cover-up. It was a Band-Aid stuck over something that needed real healing. I had no clue what was coming next. No idea that I was about to get pulled into something way darker. I was about to get sold sanity by the devil.

THREE

What the hell? Insanity and all-out chaos swirl in front of my eyes as I get out of the car. Upwards of 25 teens are crazy dancing, racing each other, and running around swinging monkey-fist necklaces. It's mischief and hoopla on steroids. Laughter and shouts blend together in an uncontrolled uproar of uncontained energy and excitement. It's contagious and intoxicating. And I want it. I want it to overtake me and pull me in. I want to belong to it. I want to belong. Period.

And it gets better. Out of the dust and mayhem in the field, three beautiful girls start to walk my way. I swear they're enrobed in light. It transfixes me, though short-lived, as a screechy little voice inside my head starts to dig at me. *Surely, someone must be standing behind you. Those goddesses would never walk up to you. You're just redneck trailer trash.*

Daryl is standing beside me and makes a move forward, nudging me to follow.

We walk a few steps and come face to face with the three god-desses. Envy floods through my body as I watch Daryl hug each of the girls. And then, out of nowhere, one of them smiles at me. *Oh, fuck!*

"Hey there. I'm Jenna. You must be a newcomer."

No words. No freaking words come out of my mouth. I can't even move my mouth. *Is she really speaking to me?*

Daryl comes to my rescue. "This is Corey. He's a good guy."

I manage a smile as my face blushes, and I struggle to find my voice. "Yeah. I'm a newcomer."

Jenna moves in close to me. Now, my heart is pounding in my chest. She leans in and reaches her arms around me. With my usual jerky movement, I throw my arms around her. We hug. Maybe I hug a little too much.

As we release each other, Jenna gives me a big smile. "Well, Corey, you're the most important person here."

I can't look at her. I hear her words, but I can't bring myself to look at her.

"Corey, you *are*! Welcome. I'm Sarah." She pushes against my body and hugs me tight. Then she makes room for Becky.

"Welcome, Corey. I'm Becky." Another warm and generous hug.

I try to process all of this welcome and acceptance and hugging. It's all smiles and happy, buy-the-world-a-Coke vibes. I notice my hands, arms, and legs are shaking. I can't stop shaking. *Fuck. I hope no one notices.*

We walk toward the field and into the wild chaos of what feels like belonging.

The intensity of the energy in the field, as we lose ourselves in all the other teens, somehow starts to calm my body. I stop shaking. In its place, I actually start to feel excitement as the rush of welcome turns into feelings of acceptance. Out of the corner of my eye, I catch two older people walking toward us. They stand out not just because of their age—probably around 19 or 20—but also because they look like clones of each other. They're both dressed in black t-shirts, faded denim jeans, and black boots. To top it off, each has long, dirty blond hair pulled back in a ponytail.

Something starts to feel a little off.

As I watch these two clones come closer, the hair on the back of my neck stands on end. I catch a glimpse of what reminds me of that drunk-on-the-glory-of-God look that some of my scary fundamentalist Christian family have. Yep. These two definitely have that I've-seen-the-light vibe going on.

They hug Daryl, Jenna, Sarah, and Becky. Then they turn all their attention to me as the others disappear. I feel awkwardly alone as I face the two pony-tailed clones. Fear starts to rumble around inside my belly.

They introduce themselves as Teddy and Nina. Then each lights up a cigarette as they tell me that they're both counselors. I can't help but notice how they smoke. They take long, deep hits. They don't waste the smoke. They hold it in and breathe it out their nostrils. They look like blond smokestacks.

I'm like a feral cat. It doesn't take much for me to get spooked and run away. I'm ready to bolt right now. But as I scope out a good escape route, I see that the others are starting to head toward Teddy and Nina, circling around and moving in close. It's like Teddy and Nina are magnets. The way they talk, smooth and inviting; the way they inhabit their bodies, confidently and calmly; the way they look at me (or anyone) as they talk, present and with a sparkle in their eyes. I can actually feel some of the energy they give off. It makes me think that they've dealt with thousands of feral cats like me before. They know how to draw us in. They know how to put us at ease. They know how to make us want to belong and to be part of their group. It's a combination of magic, moxy, and method; and it makes for a powerful brew capable of creating or destroying.

Thoughts in my head start to shout for me to get the hell out of here while I have a chance. Then, in a split second, Teddy reaches out and puts a hand on my shoulder. It's like he saw that I was about to run. With his calm and sure touch, all the shouting in my head stops. Almost like some kind of sorcery.

He moves beside me, and the next thing I know, we're all walking into a large meeting room in this hoity-toity church, on the rich side of town. This is a part of town that I never even knew existed, which isn't a big surprise given the part of town I grew up in.

I want to settle into this new space, but it's not easy. Teddy has vanished, and I'm alone. All the chaotic energy that was swirling outside is now concentrated within four walls. My eyes keep darting around, taking in all the people who are out of my league. Then I see Jenna, who is definitely out of my league. I try to wrap my head around how she didn't seem to care that I was screwed-up white trash.

"Corey!" Someone shouts from the back of the room, near the door.

As I turn around, I see Teddy and Nina. They're staring at me, flashing big, white, toothy smiles, and motioning for me to join them. I give a nod. As I start to make my way in their direction, thoughts begin to form in my mind. *What have I done wrong? Have they discovered I'm not an addict or not an addict enough? Are they going to tell me to leave?*

As soon as I'm within physical reach, they flank me. Each puts a hand on me—one on my shoulder, one over my back—as they usher me outside.

The sun is setting, flooding the tall pines with an orange light. More silence fills the outside now. I feel a churning in my stomach.

"Hey, buddy. Corey, right?" Teddy's smile starts to disarm me.

"Guys, let's sit here on the curb." Nina motions. She and I sit next to each other, while Teddy half-squats, half-kneels on the pavement in front of us.

I wait. It doesn't feel like they're going to kick me out, but something's got to be going on for them to pull me away from the others.

Teddy pulls out a cigarette and lights it up before he speaks. He's a master, it seems, of the dramatic pause. "So my man Daryl brought you here this evening. What did he tell you about us?" Teddy never breaks his look at me. He's not staring me down to win some power contest. Instead, it's as if he's extending an invitation with his look. It makes me put my guard up. Something still feels kind of off, but I can't put my finger on it.

"Not too much." My voice quivers just enough to give away any veneer of self-confidence or at-ease-ness I'm trying to communicate with my body.

"Corey, it's okay." Nina leans in as her calm voice helps me to lower my guard back down. "We're all fuck-ups here." She offers a smile, and I immediately relax.

"That's right, man. We're all royal fuck-ups here." The passion in Teddy's voice pushes in on me. "But here's the thing, Corey. We all know it. No pretending here. Hell, I love doing drugs. Heroin, coke, weed. I don't discriminate. Done 'em all, love 'em all. You know what I mean?"

Teddy flashes a smile. His question makes me nod, not just with my head but with my whole body. Teddy pauses just a little longer than needed as he takes note of my reaction.

"Corey, all of us here know what we are. We don't hide from it. We're here for each other. In this group, for each other."

Teddy takes a deep hit on his cigarette and shifts his gaze to Nina. She watches him as he pushes out the smoke from his lungs. It almost feels like a well-rehearsed move. *They're screwing each other.* The thought breaks the silence in my mind. Then Nina looks toward me and breaks the silence between the three of us.

"We understand each other. We love each other regardless of how messed up we are. I'm way messed up, Corey. I'm so much more in love with doing drugs than I could ever be in love with someone else—my family, a boyfriend, even myself. It's sick, and I know it. I just can't help it. Drugs are always there. They never let me down. They always take care of me, make me feel good. Why wouldn't I love drugs more than anyone or anything else?"

"Fucked up." Teddy puts a point on Nina's story.

"Yeah, it is. But you see, Corey, we understand each other here. Teddy understands my story. He understands me. And like I said, we love each other regardless of how messed up we are."

In the course of a few minutes, they've done it. They've found my weakness, my biggest fear, what I want more than anything in the world. They've found it.

"Corey, man, we always have room for others. We always have room for royal fuck-ups who know that they are messed up and who want to be part of what we have."

You need this. It's what you've been wanting. Make it happen. My thoughts push me past any concern for what doesn't feel quite right. My thoughts want the love drug they're offering.

Nina leans in a little closer to me. "Tell us your story, Corey." She reaches for Teddy's cigarette. "We're all messed up."

We may well have been all messed up, but I couldn't tell them my true story. I couldn't tell them about my family life. I couldn't tell them I was white trash. I couldn't tell them I lived in a trailer, in a shitty trailer park. I couldn't tell them about my drug-addicted mother or how my father hated me and was absent from my life in big ways because I disgusted him. I couldn't tell them that I wasn't an addict. Yeah, I smoked some weed on the weekend and maybe had a beer or two, but I wasn't like them. I didn't love drugs or love doing drugs. So, no, I couldn't tell them my story.

I desperately wanted to get into their group. I needed to be in the middle of all this love and all this acceptance. My desperation starts to invent an acceptable story. It kind of feels like they're playing a game with me, and I know how to play games.

So I feed them a story that feels like what they're looking for. I'm a fuck-up, just not a drug-addict fuck-up, so that's the part I beef up. I know enough about Daryl to be able to be convincing with my new story. As I come to the end of my little monologue, they both nod—first to me, then to each other.

"What a life, man. Messed up." Teddy lights up another cigarette in the midst of another one of his dramatic pauses. "Messed up."

You did it! They bought your story. My thoughts for once feel good. It feels like we're finally on the same team.

"We've all been down the road you've traveled, Corey." Nina is so good at delivery. She has real talent. She can say anything, even something as hokey and trite as what she just said, and it reels me in. I'm feeling tons of excitement that I got them to believe my big lie of a story, but I'm also feeling incredibly trusting of Nina, even though I know better. Guess it takes one to know one.

Teddy builds on Nina's words. "Corey, you're as screwed up as all of us here. I want to be real with you, man. You need help. Life isn't gonna end pretty for you if you don't get it. We know. We see it all the time. Here's the thing. We're the help you need."

After a brief pause and a steady gaze into my eyes, Teddy glances at Nina, tagging her to close the sale, so to speak.

"It's true, Corey. We don't want to see you end up dead. You're just like us. Believe me when I say that we'd be dead if we didn't have this group."

Something just happened. Nina's words got into my mind in a way that I didn't think they would. I told a story to Teddy and her. A lot of it was a lie. Fiction. But something about what she said, how she said it, is messing with my mind. Maybe I do need this group, and not just for the good feelings and the friends and the belonging. Maybe I need it because without it I will end up a drug addict. Maybe I will end up dead.

"I want to be part of this. I do. I need to be part of this group." I hear myself saying this out loud and with such conviction that I believe it. And I believe it in the way that they believe it. Something deep in the back of my mind calls out very faintly. I don't want to hear it, but it somehow breaks loose. A single chilling thought. *You just got played*.

Nina reaches an arm around me and pulls me in close as she smiles into my eyes. Teddy stands up and invites us to join him. As we stand, he puts his arms around me and hugs me close into his body. It feels so real. This is a guy who isn't afraid to hug me. His hug feels real, genuine. At that moment, I don't care what my mind is reacting to. All I know is that I need this. I need genuine emotion and caring and love for me.

Then in the afterglow of the hugs, Teddy says a few simple words in a carefree, nonchalant way. But they flood me with fear. Like the blast from a nuclear bomb right after it hits its target, his words burst into my mind and push out into my future.

"Corey, we're going to need to talk to your folks. The law re-quires us to let them know that you attended our meeting."

I'm fucked.

The single, crazy-big thought explodes in my mind. It seizes my whole body. It opens up like a trap door that I immediately fall through.

FOUR

All those little red flags I noticed that first night at the group? They were real. I didn't know it then, but my body was trying to warn me. By the time I finished talking to Teddy and Nina, it was already too late. I'd been targeted. And I fell for their love-bombing. They were part of a well-oiled machine.

I was 15. I didn't have an addiction. But none of that mattered. Teddy and Nina knew exactly what they were doing. And the truth is, there are so many teens like me—kids who don't have stable friendships or a solid place in their families. We're invisible and lonely in a bad way. That kind of emptiness turns into a quiet desperation that's hard to explain unless you've felt it. It eats away at you. And eventually, it gets so heavy that some of us start making up addiction stories just to get into a program. Not because we want recovery. We want connection. We want someone to see us. We want a place to belong.

To us, rehab looks like safety. It looks like people who care, like community, like maybe the pain will finally stop.

The treatment industry knows this. And they use it. A lot of programs out there—especially the ones chasing money—don't care if a teen really needs help. They care about filling a seat. They care about what they can bill. That's the part no one talks about: how quickly desperation becomes a sales opportunity.

Places like Enthusiastic Sobriety (founded by Bob Meehan) rarely check if someone's actually struggling with addiction.[1] That was my experience. They didn't ask the hard questions. They didn't dig deeper. If you said the right words, that was enough. That's how they got paid. And it's how kids who are scared, lonely, and desperate for connection like I was end up in these programs, completely unprepared for what comes next.

Let's pull the curtain back and take a closer look at how a typical sales process is set up to unfold in the troubled-teen industry.

If you're a parent in crisis, one of the first places you'll probably turn is the Internet. Let's say you land on the website of a treatment center. You call the number listed. Someone answers. That's considered first contact. But you're not talking to a doctor. You're not talking to a licensed therapist. In most cases, that first voice on the other end is someone in sales.

They might go by a title like "admissions coordinator" or "treatment advisor," which sounds official. It sounds like someone who knows what they're doing. Someone you can trust.

But you're not speaking with a mental-health professional. You're talking to a salesperson.

Most of the time, these people don't have any formal training in addiction, trauma, or mental health. Their job isn't to help you figure out what kind of support your child actually needs. Their job is to sell you a spot in their program. They're focused on getting a commitment from you. That's it. So instead of the conversation truly being about your family and your kid's well-being, it becomes about money for them—how much they can get from your insurance or your bank account.

Calls like these are often guided by a script. It helps the salesperson stay focused and hit the emotional points that will make you say yes. They're trained to build rapport fast, to listen for your fears, to push on the pain points. They're taught how to create urgency—like something terrible will happen if you don't take action right now. And they're often given the freedom to stretch the truth. They might tell you the program offers detox when it doesn't. Or that licensed therapists are on site when they're not. The goal isn't to offer real support. It's to get you to commit. To get the billing process started.

And just like with any sales job, there are quotas. There's pressure. A lot of these sales reps get a small base salary, but they make real money through commissions and bonuses. Some places run contests—whoever brings in the most admissions wins extra cash or a prize. And if they don't hit their numbers? They could get written up or fired. With that kind of pressure, it's not surprising that honesty starts to slip and aggressive tactics take over.

Fear is one of the most powerful tools these salespeople use. It kicks in hard when a desperate, overwhelmed parent gets on the phone with an admissions coordinator or treatment advisor. The message is clear: if you don't act right now—today—something terrible could happen. Your kid could die. Their future could be ruined. They paint a worst-case scenario and make it sound like waiting even a day could cost everything. And once that happens, it's almost impossible to think clearly. What feels like support is actually just a high-pressure sales pitch in disguise.[2]

An educational consultant, or EC, offers families another way to find their way into teen-treatment programs. Sometimes a therapist or school counselor will recommend one, or a family might come across an EC through a slick website filled with reassuring language and testimonials. Though ECs work independently, their influence is anything but small. They know the landscape inside and out: therapeutic boarding schools, residential treatment centers, wilderness programs—you name it. They present themselves as experts who can connect a teen with the "right" program. And because of that, they end up with a lot of power. Their recommendation can carry more weight than a well-designed brochure or a program director's pitch. In some ways, they're the ones quietly steering the whole industry.[3]

But with that kind of influence comes risk. ECs can charge huge fees—sometimes tens of thousands of dollars per family—and there's very little oversight in this part of the industry. That lack of accountability creates a gray area where things can get murky. Some consultants build close ties with specific programs and start funneling clients in that direction—not because it's what's best for the kid, but because there's a relationship or even money involved. On the flip side, programs rely on EC referrals to stay afloat, so they're often willing to play along. That might mean perks, special treatment, or under-the-table incentives. When that happens, the consultant's role shifts from guide to gatekeeper, and the teen—the one who actually needs help—can become an afterthought in a business transaction built on influence and favors.[4]

But it gets darker.

In some corners of the industry, there's something called "patient brokering" or "rehab surfing." It's as shady as it sounds. People with substance-use issues get moved from one program to another. The reason? It's not to help them heal, but to rack up more insurance billing. Some are even encouraged to relapse so they can re-enter treatment and start the cycle again. Every new admission means more money. I've heard of people being offered free flights, housing, or even cash to come back into treatment.[5]

It's illegal. Federal anti-kickback laws ban this kind of thing, but it still happens.[6]

Part of the reason these practices continue is that there's not much oversight. A lot of these places slip through the cracks by re-branding themselves as "sober living homes" or "wellness retreats" to get around licensing rules. Staff members who want to speak out often get shut down or reminded that the real goal is to keep the place full and the money flowing. Helping people isn't the top priority. Making a profit is.[7]

The people who pay the highest price are the ones who show up looking for help. They get stuck in a loop of empty promises, mistreatment, and relapse. Families drain their savings. Trust gets broken. And the damage erodes the entire field of addiction treatment, making it even harder for people to find real support when they need it most.

What all this really shows is that preying on desperation has become a business model. These places turn crisis into profit. They call it care, but what they're offering is pressure, manipulation, and a paycheck. And the people who are hurting most end up being treated like cash cows and walking-insurance claims.

It's a brutal system with an ugly underbelly driven by greed, masked as help. Nobody walks away untouched. And there I was, just 15 years old, about to dive headfirst into the deep end of it all, still thinking I'd found somewhere safe.

FIVE

The evening is dry and hot. I sit on the makeshift cement-block steps in front of the trailer, knees tucked into my chest. A car tears down the dirt road, kicking up a cloud of dust in its wake. The haze softens the sunlight as it drifts my way. The engine noise fades into the distance. I close my eyes and wait for the dust to reach me. Everything in me feels dry and brittle. I want to dissolve into the cloud and let it carry me away.

I try to focus on the joy and acceptance I felt that first evening at The Group. I close my eyes and press my forehead against my knees. My thoughts only swirl faster, refusing to slow down. I can't shut out the memories of everything else that happened.

It was over-the-top fun. Following the meeting, I was whisked away to an "after-meeting" hangout. I dove headfirst into a car with Jenna, Sarah, and Becky. I'm still 100% sure that they're living goddesses. We tore down the road at an insane speed and ended up at a nearby McDonald's. There, the four of us, along with Daryl and a handful of other new friends, took over the parking lot.

We hung out, chain-smoking and laughing our asses off as we ran around like unhinged hooligans. We were the loudest, rowdiest teens alive that night. Everything was fueled by a rush of love and belonging. It was a high like nothing else I'd ever felt before.

Now, on the other side of it all, it feels like torture. The Group meets this evening. In just a little while. But here I sit. Alone. I can only guess that my parents blew off Teddy and Nina. I don't know when they talked or what was said. I've barely seen my parents these past few days. My mom's been holed up in her room. She's been strung out this week. I haven't seen my dad at all. If the news had been good, surely someone would've told me. But there's been nothing. Not a word.

My cough brings me back. My lungs feel the dust now. I squint my eyes open. The dust cloud is all around me. I hear another car as it turns onto the dirt road. It will pass by soon, and a new dust cloud will get kicked up. *Move, Corey.* The thought falls away as I lower my head back onto my knees and close my eyes again. I stay put.

A moment passes, maybe two. The smell of dust in my nose begins to clear. The car's engine gets louder. I can tell that the car is slowing down. *Keep moving buddy. Nothing to see here.* The driver clearly can't read my mind. The engine roars, obnoxiously loud, and the sound shifts. It's coming toward me.

I open my eyes just as a red jeep pulls into the dirt drive that doubles as our front yard.

"Corey! Come on. Let's go!" Daryl leans out of the driver's window, hollering words like rain showering down on a dustbowl.

I'm up and in the jeep. He throws it into reverse, and spins a wheelie out of the front yard, kicking up a wild cloud of dust. It feels like I've just been sprung from jail.

"You're in, man! Teddy called and told me to come get you." A lopsided grin spreads across Daryl's face as he leans over and gives the top of my dusty head a vigorous rub.

And just like that—I'm in.

I have no idea what took place between Teddy and Nina and my parents. My gut tells me that my father was glad to hand me off to The Group. He has enough on his plate with my mother and whatever else he has going on without having to worry about me—the big disappointment in his life. I didn't give it much thought. It wasn't until years later that I became aware of all the costs that are usually involved with being accepted into such a group. And it seems that I got in all thanks to Teddy and Nina. They went to bat for me, reaching out to an EC friend of theirs who "convinced" the program director to admit me, free of charge.

I'm in! Now, my life can finally start. That's all I could think about as Daryl and I rode off into the literal sunset on the way to my first meeting as an actual participant in The Group.

From the moment I arrived that evening, I was hit with a full-on love bomb. It felt so good. I was on top of the world. I had no anxiety in my body. No fear. No isolation. Just epic love and an incredible sense of belonging. In the blink of an eye, my life flipped from something that seemed barely worth living to a dizzying rush of joy.

Now, I'm sitting in a windowless room with the door shut. It's small, but manages to fit a desk and two folding chairs. The muffled quiet inside the room gets sucked out as the door opens. Teddy and Nina strut in, flashing big white smiles and exuding easy confidence, making the room fill a little too full. They manage to squeeze themselves opposite me, with Teddy propping himself against the front of the desk and Nina sitting crosslegged on top of the desk.

All of a sudden, I feel uneasy. The small room feels tighter now, more closed in. Teddy and Nina are too close in front of me. From where I sit, in a chair that's a little too low for my long legs, they're looking down at me.

"Hey, man. Welcome! You're in." Teddy's voice is warm and enthusiastic—so much so that I half-expect him to reach out and shake my hand. But, he doesn't.

"Corey. We're family now." Nina's tone changes the energy in the room. It shifts from Teddy's upbeat welcome to something almost foreboding. It feels like a shoe is about to drop.

I shift into defense mode, tuning into all the unspoken meaning living between the lines. Their words are meant to bring me up to speed: how they talked to my father, how they managed to get him to see the truth about me, and how he wants them to take whatever steps are necessary to help me.

Can they tell my smile is fake? That I'm worried as shit right now? These are the thoughts that race through my mind. I want to be here, in the program, and their words say that they want me here, too. That they went to bat for me. *Fuck it, Corey! You've got to start trusting.*

"It's going to be work, man. But we're here for you. You gotta remember that." Teddy's words hang in the air, lingering in the silence. Both of them look at me, waiting.

"That's right, Corey. You have to trust us—me, Teddy, and everyone in The Group. Don't trust anyone else. They don't understand what you're going through. They don't know how to save you. We're the only ones, Corey. We're your family now."

What the fuck?!

"We're serious, man." Teddy's tone is firmer now. "We don't have many rules here, but this is one of them. It's that important."

I squirm in my seat. Nina and Teddy shift their bodies, too, as they get ready to punctuate the rule with surgical precision.

"Corey, you can't hang out with anyone who is not part of The Group. No one."

"Okay." My voice cracks a little. "No problem."

"No friends outside The Group. No family who's using. Your mom has a big problem. She's hooked on pills. Cut her off. No one in AA. No one in NA. No one in another treatment program. No outside therapists. No counselors. You only see counselors in The Group."

Teddy pauses to light up a cigarette. It's like he's passing the speaking stick to Nina.

"Corey, I'm actually going to be your counselor."

Somehow this all seems weirdly perfect, but the seriousness in their voices knocks me off balance. I feel like I need to respond somehow, so I blurt out as calmly and as trustingly as I can, "Right on."

Teddy takes a long drag from his cigarette, holds it for a beat, then exhales slowly, sending the smoke drifting toward the ceiling. "One more thing," he says. "No more school. It'll just get in the way of you working the program."

Shock hits me hard. My mind starts to spin. "But how do I…"

Nina cuts in gently to finish the thought for me, all while trying to steady the moment. "You don't need to worry. It's all being taken care of on our end."

That's it. Teddy and Nina get up. As they take a few steps to the door, Teddy looks back at me and calls my name. I turn my whole body to face them.

"All of us are here for you, Corey. Remember, man, we're family."

They walk out, leaving me alone in the room and staring at the blank wall.

Nina pops her head in from the side of the doorway.

"Come on, Corey! It's family time! Let's have some fun."

I jump up and rush through the door to join them. Despite my enthusiasm, I can't shake the feeling that something is off. *Are they serious?* A flicker of doubt makes me start to wonder.

Six

That first meeting with Daryl transported me into a world of connection and belonging I was desperate for. It swept me up into a whirlwind of energy spinning around with people laughing, crying, hugging like family, and swearing that sobriety was the best thing that had ever happened to them.

Getting invited to the after-meeting fun drew me in even more. It was a drug all its own. It wasn't so important where we were going, as long as I didn't have to go home. I didn't want to leave this feeling of belonging. We piled into cars, blasted music, shouted out windows, ran wild through Walmart, and eventually ended up at a McDonald's parking lot. We stayed out way too late, but I didn't care. It was all so crazy and electric. They called it recovery. To be honest, though, I would have called it an outburst of insane rowdiness. Among everyone in The Group, this was normal stuff. They even had a name for it: *sanctioned chaos*. That felt right to me. It also felt like someone finally wanted me around.

We were always told to have fun. It was like a reward for staying clean and sober. It had purpose, which made it feel okay. The more you get into it, the more it becomes the driver of the whole program. You're expected to be over-the-top loud, to be melodramatic, to hang out with people in The Group every day, all night if you could. Dropping out of school is required. Slacking off at anything is okay, and even encouraged. As long as you're with the group and not using, anything goes. The mantra becomes: as long as you're sober, it's all good. And honestly, for me, it felt liberating and exciting. We were a gang of kids doing recovery like it was a party. I loved it, even if it didn't make much sense.

But here's where it starts to get twisted. The fun didn't stay innocent for long. It turned reckless—and sometimes flat-out dangerous. I remember tearing down roads in the middle of the night with barely-legal drivers behind the wheel. I remember kids getting into fights, breaking things, trashing property. No one ever stepped in to stop us. It was all shrugged off as letting off steam, part of the "process." The more outrageous someone acted, the more praise they got. It was all a big adrenaline rush. Addictive in its own right. A high to keep chasing.

Another term I heard used to describe this wild and at times unhinged behavior was *sober insanity*. Officially, no one was drinking or doing drugs, but all the craziness was still there. All the emotional instability, all the impulsiveness, and all the melodrama.

Sometimes I wondered if it was even a bigger version of all of those things. In hindsight, it was all part of one big sinister scheme.

All the late-night chaos felt like freedom at first, but that freedom was only the beginning. It was a hook. The rules started creeping in, slowly tightening their grip. What seemed like a wild ride was actually the prelude to a different kind of control—one dressed up as care, but more about power.

People in the treatment industry toss around a lot of different terms to describe what, in reality, feels like a pretty calculated power grab—one that slowly takes over your life. It shows up in all kinds of ways. In my case, there were no papers to sign, no formal agreements or contracts. Just this constant stream of spoken rules—things I was supposed to do, but mostly things I wasn't allowed to do anymore. The to-do list was really a stop-doing list: stop hanging out with certain people, stop going to certain places, stop thinking for yourself unless it lined up with what The Group wanted.

I still get a little triggered whenever I hear phrases like *detachment for recovery* or *enforced social isolation*. These phrases may sound professional and therapeutic. But if you've been through what they're "code" for, you know what they really mean. They're just polished-up ways of describing something darker: a set of tactics that effectively erase the person entering the program.

A lot of treatment centers and recovery groups frame this kind of approach as a "clean break" or a "fresh start." They say it's necessary, even lifesaving. It's sold as something therapeutic. It's simply removing distractions so you can focus on healing. But what it usually looks like is immediate, forced separation from your entire support system. For people going into residential programs or intense behavioral-modification setups, that can mean being cut off completely from family, friends, even their own therapist.

It's pitched like a reset button, but it comes at a massive financial and emotional cost. You lose contact with the people who know you best, and suddenly, the only voices in your life are the ones running the program. Over time, it chips away at your sense of self. You start to question your own thoughts, your instincts, your memories. That isolation isn't just physical; it becomes internal. And for a lot of us, that's where the real damage begins.

For me, there really wasn't a choice. No one sat me down and said, "Here are your options." The rules were just *there*, and following them wasn't optional. It was required. That was part of the whole "onboarding process," though no one used those words. From the start, the message was loud and clear: if I wanted to get better, I had to cut ties with anyone who might "pull me back." That meant friends, sometimes family—anyone who hadn't bought into the program was labeled an enabler. Staying connected to them meant staying connected to my disease.

Looking back, it was a subtle kind of scapegoating. It shifted the blame onto people outside the program and set up this expectation where loyalty to the group became the new priority. And I didn't fight it. I remember sitting there as they explained the rules, feeling a little confused, a little thrown, but I didn't push back. I was too caught up in the warmth, the rush of being welcomed, and the fear of losing any of that. It felt like these people *got* me in a way no one else had. That kind of instant acceptance can make you want more.

I didn't feel like I was giving anything up or handing over control during the meeting. I felt like I was being let in, and it doesn't feel like a warning sign to most people. It feels like being wrapped up in love and certainty. You're told to trust the group, that they know better than you do, that this is your shot to wipe the slate clean. And when you're hurting, when you're desperate for connection, that sounds like a gift. You don't realize until much later what that "gift" actually cost.

Agreeing to the rules was treated like proof that you were serious about your recovery—like a badge of commitment. And yeah, looking back, it was a power move. Blunt, heavy-handed, and totally effective. But at the time, I didn't see it that way. I was wrecked—emotionally raw, completely cracked open, and just desperate to feel safe somewhere. I needed to belong, to feel like someone finally wanted me around. And in that state, those rules didn't feel oppressive. They felt comfortable.

It's wild to think about now, but in any other context, those rules would've sounded completely insane. Cut off your family? Stop talking to your best friend? Let strangers tell you what's best for your life? No way. But in that setting, surrounded by people who seemed to care, it felt like someone handing me a life raft. The gentle and loving way the rules were delivered was seductive. They were framed as this gift, a structure that would keep me safe. But the reality? They weren't about support. They were about control. They weren't there to care for me. They were there to make sure I didn't leave.

And here's the thing—it's not just this one group or program. This kind of forced isolation is common across a lot of settings in the addiction treatment industry. They might dress it up in therapeutic language—say it's about "disconnecting from enablers" or "focusing inward"—but the effect is the same. No matter how nicely it's worded, it's not therapy. It's control. And it shows up everywhere, from residential rehabs to behavior-modification programs, all using the same strategy: strip people of outside connections so that they'll hold on tighter to the system. And for a while, most of us do.

Just looking at the treatment industry in the U.S., one thing stands out pretty clearly: social and emotional isolation is a major part of how a lot of high-control programs operate. And it's not just a random thing. It tends to show up most in places that aren't really connected to mainstream medical or mental health systems. These programs often exist in a gray area, with little to no professional oversight.

According to the National Association of Addiction Treatment Providers (NAATP), most programs in the addiction treatment world are ethical, licensed, and above board. They usually allow regular contact with family and even encourage involvement from outside therapists—especially when recovery plans include family participation.[1] That's how it *should* work.

But right alongside those legit programs, there's a whole other side that I call "the industry." It often operates in the shadows. We're talking about unregulated, fringe setups—often tied to religious organizations, behavior-modification boot camps, or so-called "therapeutic" communities. You'll find them under all kinds of labels: residential treatment centers, therapeutic boarding schools, faith-based recovery programs, or outpatient programs that look safe on the surface but take a hard turn once you're inside.

These places tend to use this twisted logic to justify cutting people off from the outside world. They call it "protection," or "structure," or "necessary tough love"—but really, it's enforced isolation dressed up as treatment. Instead of offering support, they build walls between participants and the people who care about them, all in the name of recovery. It's an upside-down version of help, and too many people don't realize what's happening until they're already deep in it.

As I've already touched on in earlier chapters, the driving force behind a lot of these programs isn't some deep concern for people's well-being—it's money. Plain and simple. Greed is what keeps the machine running.

The sales staff—because yes, these places often have sales teams—know exactly how to work a referral. They can spot a desperate family a mile away. And that's who they go after, because it's way easier to sell a $20,000 to $60,000 treatment program (for just 30 to 90 days, by the way) when someone is terrified and looking for any shred of hope.

The standard pitch usually sounds something like this: "Your loved one is in danger. We're their only chance. But to help them, you'll need to trust us completely—which means no contact for a while." Families, overwhelmed and afraid, often agree. It sounds like tough love. It sounds like structure. But really, it's a setup. That whole idea of enforced isolation gets packaged as the key to recovery, when in reality, it's just part of the sales strategy. And for the people caught in the middle—the ones actually going through the program—it can be the beginning of a much deeper kind of harm.

When you mix a desperate family, a lack of real oversight, and the greed of the people running these programs, you get a setup that's ripe for abuse. And sadly, that's exactly what happens in a lot of these places. Enforced isolation becomes a tool—not for healing, but for control.

From the inside, as a participant, you're told your family is part of your problem. That they represent your "disease." From the outside, the family is told that their involvement might actually get in the way of treatment. It creates this wedge—one that's carefully and intentionally driven in to separate people from their support systems.

And here's the kicker: the more control the program or facility gets, the more money they can make. It's a system that thrives on cutting people off and making them completely dependent on the group or the facility. The tighter the grip, the longer someone stays—and the higher the bill climbs.

Coercion and manipulation are baked into how enforced isolation works in these kinds of programs. It simply doesn't happen without them. But to get families on board early, the messaging is dressed up in calm, clinical language. During the sales pitch, it usually sounds like *"We recommend a period of disconnection."* That phrasing feels gentle, even thoughtful—like it's part of a carefully considered therapeutic plan.

But once the participant is actually in the program, that language changes fast. Suddenly, it's not a recommendation anymore. It's a rule. Families are told *"We require that you stop contact."* And by that point, it's too late. Longtime therapists who may have worked with the participant for years are now considered part of the "old system." Any concern voiced by a parent is rebranded as enabling.

It's shocking for families, but they often go along with it—because they're exhausted, scared, and already being warned that *any* outside interference could lead to relapse or worse. The staff doesn't say it outright, but the implication is clear: if your kid dies, it might be because *you* didn't let us do our job. That kind of fear shuts people down fast.

By then, the trap has already been set. Everyone—parents, siblings, even the participant—is told to "trust the process." That phrase gets repeated so often it starts to feel like gospel. But what it really means is don't ask questions, don't push back, and definitely don't reconnect with the people who might remind you who you were before all this started.

In a lot of inpatient programs like these, contact with the outside world basically disappears. Most patients aren't allowed to make phone calls at all. If they are allowed, the calls are closely monitored and usually kept short. Letters? Usually discouraged—and if one actually gets through, staff will read and censor it. Therapy with

anyone outside the program? Not a chance. Everything is tightly controlled, and the message is clear: the only people you
should be talking to are *us*.

All of this isolation is framed as part of the "healing process,"
but what it really leads to is something called *re-socialization*.
What does that mean in plain English? It means the patient
starts depending entirely on the program—on the staff, the
group, the rules. It doesn't matter if the program is in a rehab
center, a boarding school, or someone's living room. The person's identity gets so stripped down that they start to rebuild
themselves based on the group's approval and expectations.
Their sense of self is so shaken that clinging to the program
starts to feel like the only way to survive.

This isn't just emotional control. It's emotional captivity.
The ability to think and feel for yourself gets hijacked. And
trauma-informed experts emphasize that this kind of isolation
can actually do way more harm than good—especially for people with trauma histories. These experts point out that cutting
people off from their established supports is often re-traumatizing. It mirrors the dynamics of abuse: isolation, control, and
gaslighting under the guise of help.[2]

That's the part that's so insidious. It's not just that you're being
controlled—it's that it's all being sold as love, healing, and care.

But for many people, it ends up feeling more like another form of harm disguised as recovery.

The mechanisms that these programs use to guarantee social isolation are straight-up coercive. They use threats, intimidation, and manipulation. Whether these show up as being obvious and out in the open or sneaky and subtle, coercion is always lurking in the background. It's what keeps the control and dependence locked in.

A classic example is the threat of getting kicked out of the program—but only after you've already been made emotionally dependent on it. That's not just bad luck; it's a trap, a way to keep people vulnerable so the program can keep its grip. And getting expelled at that point? It doesn't mean you just go home. It means you're pushed into a world where every safety net is gone. No place to live, no insurance, no family support, no friends, no skills—just the cold message of "You chose relapse over recovery."

This kind of psychological manipulation sends another brutal message: love and acceptance aren't unconditional. They are rewards you have to earn, and then lose at the drop of a hat. For many people, it reopens old wounds—abandonment, rejection, co-dependency—and can actually re-traumatize them. It's like weaponizing the very things they're already struggling with.

Back in 2019, a big investigation by Reveal—the Center for Investigative Reporting—pulled back the curtain on just how far some addiction treatment programs will go to keep control over their participants.[3] One of the programs they looked into was the Cenikor Foundation, a well-known nonprofit based in Texas. What they uncovered was pretty shocking.

Cenikor had this practice where participants were made to work unpaid for huge companies like Shell Oil, Walmart, and Exxon. We're talking about long, grueling days—building oil rigs, working construction, or hauling things around warehouses. After ten-hour shifts, these folks would just go back to the facility to crash and start all over again the next day. The program sold it as part of their "discipline and rehabilitation" plan.

Everything was run on a strict behavioral hierarchy, and contact with anyone outside the program—family included—was tightly controlled. Participants who struggled or failed to comply could set themselves up to be punished in ways that included expulsion or labor reassignment. Many critics described the program as indentured servitude sold as therapy.

Not every program forces people into unpaid labor, but coercion is still a big part of how social isolation gets started and keeps going. That was definitely true in my experience—it's one of the very first things the program does once you're accepted.

If you spend any time in anonymous online recovery forums, you'll see a lot of people sharing similar stories. They talk about being told to block phone numbers, delete social media accounts, and stop writing or receiving letters. Reading through those posts, it's clear these actions don't just take away your freedom—they chip away at your sense of self and identity.

One former participant reportedly put it this way: "I didn't talk to my mom for a year. I thought I was doing the right thing, and I wasn't even given the option to say no. They told me she was enabling me just because she cried on the phone." That kind of control runs deep, and it's one of the toughest parts to come back from.[4]

American Addiction Centers is one of the biggest rehab networks across the U.S., and they've put out an article called *Communicating with a Loved One in Rehab*. It explains what families can expect when a loved one is in the first few weeks of treatment. According to the article, communication will be "very limited" because the person needs to focus all their energy on getting better.[5]

That might sound reasonable on the surface, and it's not exactly wrong. But honestly, it kind of sugarcoats what actually happens in a lot of programs. Once someone starts treatment, the rules around communication can feel more like strict bans than gentle limits. Family visits get denied. Phone calls go unanswered. And when families finally get to ask questions, they often hear something vague like "They're still adjusting."

It's a polite way of shutting loved ones out, and that can be really hard for families to deal with.

Some psychologists have pointed out that these high-control treatment programs operate on a totally distorted logic—they flip reality upside down. They label natural things like grief as "enabling" and genuine concern as "codependency." It's a way to rewrite the rules so they can justify controlling almost every part of a participant's life, sometimes in ways that border on abuse.[6]

The first step is deciding which relationships are "good" and which are "bad." If a relationship supports the program's agenda, it's healthy and good. If it challenges the program's authority, it's automatically unhealthy and bad. Then any emotional reactions that don't fit the program's narrative get pathologized—basically, seen as problems. If a participant starts questioning all this, they're branded as "resistant."

Outside therapy is often seen as a threat, so when someone enters the program, they're usually told to cut ties with any therapists they were seeing before. Even though suddenly dropping a therapeutic relationship with a trained professional can be harmful, it's often spun as a way to show trust in the program and its staff.

When you look at these tactics, it's easy to see why so many people compare certain addiction treatment programs to cults. The overlap is pretty clear.

What makes this whole approach even more messed up is that while these programs cut people off from family and friends—supposedly to keep them safe and ensure successful treatment—they sometimes turn a blind eye to alcohol and drug use happening among the participants themselves. It's the last thing you would expect from a place that's supposed to be about recovery.

SEVEN

The whole of my parent's trailer could fit inside this room. I'm sure of it. I stand there frozen for a beat, trying to take it all in. Tyler's house, and especially this swanky living room, is massive. The ceiling with its dark exposed beams stretches high above my head. Light filters in through the windows and catches the shiny paneled walls, which give way to built-in bookcases packed with books, twin fireplaces, and a wall of smug family portraits of perfect people with perfect smiles.

Two black leather sofas sit like anchors around glass tables topped with fresh flowers. In the corner, a seriously well-stocked bar shows off with tall, fancy-shaped liquor bottles and crystal tumblers that sparkle. A deep chime rings out and draws my attention to the grandfather clock on the far side of the room. The rich sound sinks into my chest. For a second it seems like the tic-tocs of the clock are measuring more than time. I feel like they're quietly counting down how long I'll be allowed to stay on this side of the tracks in this fancy world.

It's 10 a.m., and Tyler's parents are off at work. I bet they're doctors, maybe lawyers. Whatever they do, it clearly pays. People like them, along with their perfectly posed relatives on the wall, have never had to use food stamps.

Sam is already sprawled out on the floor, his back resting against one of the leather sofas like he owns the place. He looks totally at ease, like this kind of luxury is just normal. Tyler drops down beside him and gestures for me to join them on the floor. I follow his lead and lower myself onto the thick carpet, trying to get comfortable. As I settle in, a random thought floats through my head: *Why the hell are we all sitting on the floor when there are plush, expensive chairs all around us?*

Sam and Tyler, only a few weeks ahead of me in the program, have been assigned as my mentors. They're the ones who will show me how things work, keep me social, make sure I stay clean. They're mid-conversation, still talking about the same thing they've been dissecting since we walked in. Something about a girl getting caught hanging out with friends who aren't in The Group. Their words bounce back and forth, but I'm not really following.

My focus keeps drifting. The way the light pours into the room makes it feel even bigger, more unreal. And then, out of nowhere, I'm not there anymore—I'm back home, staring down at the cracked linoleum in our trailer's kitchen, scraping the last bit of peanut butter from the jar. My mind spins. Thoughts fly around, jabbing me from every angle. Tyler's got everything—this mansion, money, parents with real careers. And me? I've got this constant stream of anger, fear, and insecurity. I'm part of The Group now, yeah. But what I want more than anything at this moment is to fit in. My sense of belonging is still kind of a moving target.

Then—

"Corey!"

Hearing my name jolts me out of my mind trip.

They're both looking at me, grinning like they're in on a joke that I missed.

"Kind of jumpy there, aren't you?" Tyler says, his voice loose and unfocused, like he's halfway here and halfway floating somewhere else.

Sam leans over and gets in my face. "Thinking about something off-limits?" His eyes dance about. Something daring lurks underneath his question. Like he's testing the water.

Something in me wants to punch him. I want to knock that look off his face. But I don't. I laugh. Fake. Loud. Like I'm in on whatever game this is supposed to be. "It's all I think about." I shoot back with a sarcastic grin. "I mean, isn't that basically what we all do?"

Sam howls with laughter. "Facts!" he shouts.

Tyler chuckles too, sinking deeper into the carpet. That's when I notice—his eyes are glassy and red, his eyelids heavy.

"You're high," I blurt out before I can stop myself.

Sam's eyes shift to Tyler, then back to me, like he's waiting to see how this plays out.

Tyler shrugs. "A little."

I keep my face calm, but my whole body tenses. I can't tell if I'm buzzing from the thrill of being let in on something secret or pissed off that I'm part of some kind of lie.

Tyler doesn't blink. "Chill, Corey. It's just a little weed."

Sam jumps in without missing a beat. "No one's clean all the time. You learn to work the system. It's almost too easy."

He says it like gospel—like he's quoting scripture from some twisted recovery Bible.

"You guys are supposed to be my mentors." My voice shows more alarm than I wanted it to.

Tyler rolls onto his side, propping his head up casually, like we're just hanging out and everything's fine. Sam doesn't miss a beat. "And we *are* doing our job. We're showing you how it *really* works."

Tyler nods, calm as ever. "You just gotta keep your story straight. That means, yeah, sometimes you gotta lie."

Then, like some magical TV moment, Tyler reaches under the sofa and pulls out a bottle of whiskey. It's sleek and curved, with gold trim on the label that catches the light just right. He unscrews the top like it's nothing and takes a long swig straight from the bottle. *He takes a drink from the fucking bottle.* That's all I can hear in my mind as I watch him tip the bottle back with zero hesitation. Then he passes it over to Sam, who does the same.

Now, the bottle gets offered to me. Sam's arm outstretched. The bottle hangs there between us, like a dare. The longer I hesitate, the more the dare turns into an invitation. A way in. And suddenly, I see it for what it is. I'm not just going along with something. I'm being let in. I'm *belonging*.

I take the bottle.

Sam grins, and in that moment, he welcomes me in a way that I haven't felt before. "Dude, we're not gonna narc on you," he says. "We're all in this together."

I take a swig. It burns my throat as I hand the bottle off to Tyler, trying to keep my expression unreadable, cool.

"That's right, Corey." Tyler slurs his words. "This is what it means to be in The Group. The staff—people like Teddy and Nina—they just want your butt in a seat."

Another handoff and Sam says the magic words. "We actually care about you. The staff only see dollar signs. We don't care if you're rich or broke-ass poor. We love you, man."

Then he pulls me into a bear hug. It's tight and warm and surprisingly real. And just like that, my mind quiets down. No noise about my mom. No thoughts about the trailer. No shame. No rules. Just silence. Like everything inside me finally takes a breath.

I don't feel like I'm falling short anymore. I don't feel scared. I just feel good.

As Sam and I pull apart, Tyler chimes in. "You think they're all clean, man?"

I don't answer. I don't want to. I just want Tyler to shut up so I can stay in this strange kind of comfort.

He takes my silence as a yes. "Please," he mumbles. Then he drifts off completely.

Sam looks at Tyler, then turns to me. "Corey, The Group's just an act. A performance. Say the right thing, look the part, and boom! You're a success story. They call you a winner."

And honestly, I've already started to feel it. I haven't been in The Group long, but I've caught on fast. Sitting here, breaking the rules with Sam and Tyler should have me on edge, should make me feel guilty. But that's not what's happening. I feel safe. Like I'm finally in on the secret. Like I've figured out how to win at the game, and my new mentors are the ones handing me the cheat codes.

Sam leans back on his elbows. "All you gotta do is lie when you have to. Smile pretty when they ask. Keep your head down. Don't cause trouble."

I nod. Part of me knows I'm being pulled into something twisted, and I should probably be scared. But I'm not. I almost laugh out loud. It's so messed up. But it also feels so good. I've never felt this kind of belonging before. The idea of ratting them out? Of blowing this up? No way. That would mean losing everything I've finally just found.

This kind of connection is what I've wanted all along. I can't overthink it. If I do, the fear starts to creep back in. And yeah, part of me knows this isn't real. But another part doesn't care. Not even a little.

"Shit." Sam taps my shoulder hard and I snap to attention. Tyler's out cold and has pissed on himself.

"Fuck," Sam mutters, half-panicked.

Panic bubbles up in me, too, but underneath is something else: a strange, twisted kind of loyalty. We both jump into action and into the belonging.

EIGHT

Let's call it what it really was: a lack of sincerity. That's the polite version, anyway. In reality, it was everywhere in The Group. And the more I've seen since, the more I realize it wasn't just our group. It's something that runs through the recovery industry like a bad current. And I was right in the thick of it. From the moment I sat down with Teddy and Nina, I became part of the game.

Here's one thing I'll say with total confidence: most of the kids in my group were full of shit—just like I was. They didn't have drug problems. Half of them didn't even know what real drugs were. A lot had sniffed glue, done a few whippets, maybe lied about drinking. That was it. But they had money, they had privilege, and they had wild ideas about what being "cool" or "hardcore" was supposed to look like. So they made stuff up. They told elaborate stories about blacking out, about chaos and destruction, about things they probably never actually did. In the program, we even had a name for it: *war stories.* But most of it? Total BS. And you could tell. We were just kids pretending to be people with pasts we didn't have.

What still blows my mind is how easily the adults bought into it. A lot of us had uptight or super religious parents, so it didn't really matter how crazy our stories sounded—the second they heard "drugs" or "drinking," they freaked out. But the staff? The counselors? How did none of them question what was going on? How did they not see through it?

To be fair, programs like the one I was in do have people who are truly struggling with addiction. There are people who show up ready to face themselves and get help. That part is real and important to acknowledge. But it's also part of what makes these programs so complicated. Because when you mix in people who don't actually have addiction issues, the whole thing gets messy.

As strange as it sounds, there's a growing body of evidence—and plenty of personal stories—that show programs meant to treat addiction can actually create it in some cases. For kids like me, being in that environment didn't steer us away from drugs. It often pulled us closer. We learned to lie better. We picked up the language of addiction. Some of us even started using substances (or using them more) *because* we felt we had to live up to the stories we told.

At the core of most addiction recovery programs is this idea of community—of people healing together. Whether it's group therapy, 12-step meetings, or living in shared spaces, the setup is all about connection. You're supposed to support each other, learn from one another's stories, and build a kind of chosen family. And when it works, it *can* be powerful.

But there's a darker side to all of it that becomes a tradeoff that not many people talk about. These same environments can also become the perfect breeding ground for toxic behaviors.

Dr. Gabor Maté, a well-known voice in the addiction space, talks about this a lot. He says addiction isn't just about chemical dependency. It's a coping mechanism, rooted in pain, trauma, and unmet emotional needs.[1] According to him, when people who are already struggling mentally or emotionally get placed into environments where manipulation, lying, and even drug use are quietly normalized, they're far more likely to adopt those behaviors. And honestly? That's exactly what happened to me.

Within weeks of joining The Group, I was smoking weed, snorting coke, and getting trashed on some seriously good liquor. Before that, I didn't even know what coke *was.* But to me, all of it felt like a badge of honor. Like I'd finally arrived—finally escaped the trailer parks and "white-trash" label I'd been carrying. I thought I'd found my people. People who saw me and still accepted me. That feeling of belonging? That's a powerful drug all on its own.

Anyone who spends even a little time in group therapy notices something right away: there's this constant push and pull between people. You're supposed to be processing your pain and learning from others, but there's this weird competition happening beneath the surface. Everyone's trying to stand out, craving some kind of validation through the stories they share.

So you quickly learn to tell war stories about how wild or messed up your past was. And if you didn't have a big, dramatic story? You basically disappeared. It was like you didn't matter. So what happens? People start exaggerating. Embellishing. Straight-up making things up. And in some cases, they start *living out* the stories they feel pressured to tell.

That's the real danger. Because in those spaces, drama equals approval. And before you know it, people are being rewarded for lying—and even worse, for putting themselves in harm's way just to fit in.

Most of what happens in addiction treatment settings feels intense—like everything is dialed up a notch. One of the strongest dynamics at play is social learning. It's just how we work as people: we watch, we absorb, we copy. In any new environment, we look to those who've already figured out how things work. That's how we learn to fit in.

In recovery programs, especially for teens and young adults who come in without much real experience with addiction, this can have devastating effects. Newcomers walk into this tight-knit culture of recovery and find that it's filled with group lingo, dramatic stories, and a host of unspoken rules. What becomes obvious to the newcomers is that they're surrounded by people who already know how to navigate it. So what do they do? They start observing. They watch how people act, what people say, and what gets attention or praise. And then, pretty quickly, they start mimicking the culture.

Here's the scary part: a lot of what gets modeled isn't healthy. Some of it's downright dangerous. Newcomers see others lying to therapists, gaming the system, faking drug tests, and making up war stories. And they see those behaviors *working*. They see how the behaviors can be used to get sympathy, credibility, and even praise. So those same tactics spread and become a kind of survival skill.

This idea isn't new. Back in the '70s, psychologist Albert Bandura came up with the theory of social learning, which basically says we learn behavior by watching others and copying what gets rewarded.[2] And that's exactly what you see in these programs. Manipulation, exaggeration, even real drug use—all start to feel like the cost of belonging.

I've heard so many people say the same thing: "If you didn't act the part, it was like you weren't serious about recovery." That pressure is real. In my case, I actually started using more drugs (and more serious drugs) just to fit in and to prove I belonged.

And it's not just anecdotal. A 2021 study in *Health Affairs* found that some residential addiction treatment programs in the U.S. admit people without even checking if they actually meet the criteria for substance use treatment.[3] That's a huge red flag. What ends up happening is that people who don't need treatment for substance use are getting pulled into these treatment programs. Then, while in the programs, they start picking up harmful behaviors *because* of the environment. It's a risky situation, and it's happening way more often than most of us would expect.

In psychology, terms like *observational learning* and *modeling* get used to explain why people (especially non-addicts) start mimicking addictive or manipulative behaviors in treatment settings. But really, it boils down to something simple: we're wired to copy the people around us. It's human nature.

Dr. Steven Hayes, a well-known psychologist and creator of Acceptance and Commitment Therapy (ACT), talks about this a lot. He explains that our drive to imitate others is baked into our evolutionary survival instincts. When we're dropped into situations that feel uncertain or stressful—like a rehab program, for example—we naturally look around and start copying the people who seem to belong. We do what they do, especially if it earns social approval or makes us feel more secure.[4]

So, as soon as someone without a history of addiction walks into a recovery program and sees that things like drug use, manipula-

tion, or exaggerating your story are normalized or even rewarded, they often start doing the same. Not necessarily because
they want to, but because fitting in feels like a lifeline.

This pressure gets worse because addiction is often framed in
really black-and-white terms. It's often said in recovery circles
that addiction is like being pregnant—you either are or you
aren't. There's rarely any space for nuance. And when addiction becomes tied to identity, it can push people to take on
behaviors they wouldn't have considered before, just to prove
they belong. If you don't have a dramatic story, you might start
making one up—or worse, start living one out.

The bottom line is that the need to feel accepted, especially
in a place as emotionally intense as treatment, can push people
to behave in ways they might never have considered. It's a hard
truth, and it's one we need to talk about more openly.

We need to shine some light on another part of this dynamic:
the staff. The phrase *the fox guarding the henhouse* is a pretty
spot-on way to describe how a certain part of the addiction
treatment industry handles staffing.

Many treatment centers *do* have licensed clinicians on staff.
That's important to acknowledge. But here's what doesn't get
talked about enough: a big chunk of the day-to-day work that is
hands-on and patient-facing is often left to behavioral techs or peer

recovery coaches. And a lot of these folks may be in the early stages of their own recovery journeys.

That's where things can go off-track. These staff members are often not trained (or barely trained) to spot signs of manipulation, relapse, or other harmful behaviors, let alone intervene in a meaningful way. So you end up with people in positions of authority who might not be equipped to handle the very issues they're supposed to be managing.

Now, lived experience can be incredibly valuable in recovery spaces—no question. But without proper oversight and training, it can also become a real liability. When staff don't have the skills or confidence to set boundaries or clinically manage toxic behavior, the whole environment suffers. And that's how the fox ends up guarding the henhouse door.

Survivors continue to come forward with their stories about how a lot of staff in the industry haven't been trained to recognize or respond to unhealthy behaviors as they surface. Even worse, some actually have ended up reinforcing those behaviors. Why? Burnout is part of it. But another alarming factor is that many of them are still in recovery themselves and feel uncomfortable "policing" others in the same boat. And a lot of the "therapists" working with teens or adults in the treatment industry aren't actually licensed.[5] From what I've seen—and discovered in my own research—they're more like interns, still working toward their credentials.

It's a dynamic that raises serious questions about safety, accountability, and what "help" is supposed to look like.

NINE

All I can see are his eyes. That's it. Tunnel vision. Just his angry eyes locked on me. The rest of the room fades out. My body feels tight, like everything's closing in on itself.

"Do you hear me, Corey?"

His voice breaks into the silence. It cuts through, sharp and heavy with frustration. Teddy's words fill the room with the weight of his disappointment and anger. I want to respond, but nothing comes out. I feel frozen.

"Are you gonna cry now?"

I feel my eyes start to sting. Tears form. I don't want them to fall out of my eyes, but everything in me is stirred up: fear, anger, shame, sadness. I look weak, but I can't stop the tears. *Say something goddamnit!* This doesn't feel right.

"Cry like a pathetic little baby. It's not gonna change anything. Like I said, you're out. No contact with anyone in The Group. You're a nobody now. You fucked up. It's all on you, Corey. I hope you don't fuck up again and get yourself killed."

I finally open my mouth to push back, but Teddy cuts me off.

"Leave, Corey. Now."

I get up and head for the door.

"Where do you think you're going, Corey?"

"You told me to leave."

"That's right. But you don't get to leave the way you came in." Teddy nods toward a door I hadn't noticed before. It's off to the left, behind the little desk in this cramped room. "That's the door for fuck-ups. The door for people who screw up and can't take their own life seriously enough to follow the rules. That's your door."

I feel Teddy drilling down on me with his look. I feel pinned down, little, worthless. I can't even bring myself to look up.

I turn, try to move fast, but my feet catch on each other. I stumble. My chest tightens. I can't breathe. *Fuck. I can't breathe!* I push the door open and lunge into the warm evening air.

It hits me like a wave. It flows into my lungs, part of a world that suddenly feels too big, too alone, and too scary.

I don't deserve this. I toss and turn, sweaty and wide awake, stuck in the middle of another sleepless night. I keep replaying everything in my head, which isn't much. That's part of what makes me so mad. I don't know anything. I'm confused and frustrated.

I trusted my mentors. I trusted The Group. We were all living double lives, all good at saying the right things and hiding the rest. But we were there for each other. We were family, at least that's what I thought.

The sleepless nights blur into long, empty days, and those days start stacking into weeks. Fear grows stronger and becomes the only measure in my life. My world feels jagged. I'm alone. None of my friends from The Group—not a single one of them—calls me. It's as if they never existed. It's like they all died. No funeral. No nothing. Just gone.

Time doesn't feel real anymore. The minutes and hours bleed into each other. Formless and heavy. I don't have school, or work, or friends. There's nothing pulling me forward. All I can do is sit with myself. And the longer I sit, the more I start to break down. *Who am I without my friends? Without The Group?*

And now, in the harsh light of a morning that's already too hot, a way too big realization gut punches me: *Maybe I did fuck up. Maybe it really is my fault. Somehow I must have hurt The Group. Let everyone down.* Shame creeps in as I clearly start to see that they were trying to help me, and I fucked it up.

Tears stream down Melissa's cheeks as she buries her face in her hands. The room is empty now. She's alone in the circle of chairs pushed up against the walls. The rest of the therapy group is gone. Melissa knows that she did what she had to do. She had to tell her counselor something. She had to cry. Her performance needed to be dramatic enough to look like she was working the program. Deep down, Melissa didn't want to hurt anyone, but she couldn't risk getting kicked out.

She knew, like everyone knows, tears and big emotions are required—fake or real, they're required during group therapy.

Now, after her fake tears, in the quiet of the room, real tears flood her eyes. They look the same as those she shed during the group session, but they feel so different. She hates herself. She hates what her story and her performance during the therapy session are going to do to Corey. Now, her tears align with her heart. The shame that they betray is real. Her hatred for herself is real.

She's safe for now. She's still in The Group for now. (Later, her parents will be told she needs an expensive in-patient program or she's out for good.)

❖

"What do you mean?" I hear myself yell as I get in Tyler's face.

"Dude, chill," he says, backing up a little. "You can't be here. And who's that in the driveway? You know my parents can't know I'm talking to you."

I glance over my shoulder at the beat-up truck idling in the driveway. My messed-up uncle and his girlfriend gave me a lift on their way to a painting job.

"Why would she say that?" I whip my head back toward Tyler. "Why would she throw me under the bus like that?"

"I don't know, Corey. It was her turn to talk in group. Maybe she panicked. Got desperate. But you gotta go, man. My mom's gonna be home any minute."

"How could she do that?" I say, my voice rising. "She got me kicked out of The Group. What the fuck!"

"You know the rules. No sex with group members."

"But we didn't have sex!"

"Whatever, Corey. She told a different story."

"Fuck!" I scream out long and loud.

A car horn blares. "Corey! Let's go!" It's my uncle yelling from the truck.

"You gotta go," Tyler says. "If anyone finds out we talked, I'm next. Don't get me kicked out, too."

Another long and excruciating day blurs into another sleepless night. I keep fixating on how Melissa narced on us. She had to have lied. It's all so fucked up.

I roll over and squeeze my eyes shut, trying to block out the thoughts spinning in my mind. But they keep coming. Now with images, doubts, questions. All circling each other like they're feeding off the chaos. I flip onto my back. My eyes snap open.

Maybe it is all on me. Maybe I did ruin everything. I don't know if I was wrong or if I was wronged. I don't even trust myself anymore. The only thing I do know is that I was hoping we would hook up. I can admit that. Maybe that was why I got kicked out.

I shut my eyes again, tighter this time as I try to stop the next wave of thoughts before it hits. *If I did screw up, I need to make amends somehow. I'll do whatever it takes to get back in. I can confess to whatever they want me to confess to. Whatever it takes. I just need to get back in. Because being out? Being cut off like this? I can't take it.*

I walk through the main room. Everyone looks at me out of the corner of their eyes. They mumble to each other. No one says a word to me. They don't have to.

Just as I'm turning the corner to go to the office, I literally run into Teddy. We both take a step back. His coffee sloshes out of the cup and splashes onto his light-blue T-shirt. His face tightens with annoyance, but then shifts as he recognizes me. Now, it's something colder and more calculated.

He puts his cup of coffee on a small table, freeing up his hands. I can tell what's coming.

"Get out, Corey," he says. His words are low and restrained. They still cut into me though.

I feel myself turn red from embarrassment. Everyone's watching. My voice is shaky and cracks as it comes out of my mouth. "Teddy, can we go into the office and talk?"

"No, we can't. You need to leave." His tone is flat and emotionless. "This isn't a place for failures."

Fuck it. I don't care who sees. "Please, Teddy. I'll do whatever it takes. I know I fucked up. I'm sorry. I won't do it again." Tears start to pour out of my eyes. I can't control them. *I'm such a fucking loser.*

I realize my whole body is shaking. Teddy just watches me. Then, I see it. His body shifts. It relaxes. Like a bully realizing he's got complete control over some weak fuck.

Tunnel vision hits. It's just me and him now. His eyes lock on mine. It's like he's daring me to keep groveling.

Then he speaks loud enough for everyone in the room to hear.

"Do you think it's fair to let you back in after you let everyone down, especially Melissa? Tell me, Corey. Why should I let you back in?"

I'm silent as I listen to the translation of his words inside my head. *You are weak and pathetic, Corey. Beg for this. Beg to get back in. Beg for another chance at life.*

TEN

I still remember standing outside in the warm evening air, just staring at the closed door I'd walked through minutes earlier. The world suddenly felt way too big, but it was still pressing in on me from all sides. I'd just been kicked out of the program, and all I could do was stare at that door because everything I thought I had, everything that felt like my life, was on the other side of it.

Looking back now, I was in mental, emotional, and physical shock. It was like my body had shut down. And the sad truth is, this kind of thing happens all the time in the treatment industry. One minute you're "part of the community," and then the next minute you're standing outside with whatever belongings you have, completely dazed and not sure where to go.

The official term for it is *behavioral discharge*. It sounds clinical. But let's call it what it is: an emotional gut-punch. A lot of places in this industry use public shaming and rejection instead of support when someone relapses or breaks a rule. They say things like "we don't coddle weakness." Then, just like that, you're out.

The whole thing leaves you stunned. Betrayed. Humiliated. And here's the messed-up part: even after all that, a lot of us—myself included—still find ways to defend the very program that turned its back on us. That's how strong the grip can be.

You don't hear about these stories nearly as much as you should. Even though there are tons of people in recovery who've been kicked out of abusive or controlling treatment programs, their experiences often go unreported. The psychological damage that follows can be brutal—confusing, deeply painful, and sometimes even deadly.

When these stories do come out, it's usually in quiet places like in survivor groups, trauma-informed therapy sessions, spaces where people finally feel safe enough to speak. And what's really striking is how often survivors feel a kind of loyalty to the very programs that hurt them. It doesn't make logical sense, but that's part of the pain. It mirrors the same dynamic as Stockholm syndrome.

In those hostage situations, people form emotional bonds with their captors. And we're now seeing similar patterns in certain rehab settings, especially the more punitive, high-control residential programs. These places talk a big game about healing and transformation—but more often than not, it's a promise that gets used as leverage. You're expected to follow every rule without question, open up on command, and fall in line with whatever the program says is "the right way" to recover.

And the way they enforce it can be heartless and coercive. Programs use public shaming in front of the group, cutting you off from your family or friends, constantly reminding you that you could be kicked out at any moment. It's less about support and more about control. It creates this huge imbalance of power where the participants start feeling like they *need* the program, even when it's hurting them. Over time, it becomes a twisted kind of attachment. People end up emotionally tied to the very thing that broke them down.

A lot of these programs talk about *tough love*—something that traces back to the early days of 12-step recovery. Back then, it was more about people voluntarily coming together, admitting they were struggling, and supporting each other through surrender and honesty. But what we see now in the treatment industry is very different.

Instead of a peer-led, voluntary model, we've got a system that's often powered by court mandates, family pressure, or insurance money. This results in a host of programs that lean hard into punishment instead of healing. They act like they're helping, but they're often just enforcing control. There's no real oversight in place. This puts professional ethics on shaky ground and opens the door wide to harsh punishments for anyone who doesn't fall in line.

Dr. Jennifer Freyd is a psychologist and Professor Emerit of Psychology at the University of Oregon who has done important work on betrayal trauma. Her research shows that people who experience abuse in high-control environments (like some of these rehab programs) can actually form emotional bonds with the very people or systems that hurt them. It's called *trauma bonding*, and it can distort your perception of what's healthy, making it difficult to recognize abuse. Trauma bonding makes you feel like you're tearing apart your whole sense of identity if you betray the program.[1] This dynamic shows up way too often in questionable treatment centers and easily opens the door to manipulation and deep psychological harm.

When someone's ability to recognize the harm they're experiencing gets distorted, it can lead to a dangerous outcome: they start forming emotional attachments to the very people or systems that are hurting them. Psychiatrist and trauma expert Bessel van der Kolk explains that trauma can create disorganized attachment, causing survivors to feel compelled to stay connected to the very people or systems that are hurting them, even when it is harmful, in order to survive.[2]

It's a scary truth, especially when you think about how many people enter recovery programs already carrying trauma from unstable or abusive relationships. When they land in a program that uses manipulation, shame, and unpredictable approval to control people, it can feel disturbingly familiar. And instead of feeling safe, participants start falling back into old survival habits and do whatever it takes to stay in the good graces of the people in charge. Not because they feel supported, but because they're terrified of rejection. Their attachment isn't rooted in trust. It's rooted in fear.

So what happens when someone gets kicked out? It's often sudden and harsh, with no resources, no warning, and no place to go. The person loses their sense of community and sometimes even their housing. Retraumatization becomes almost inevitable. And here's the heartbreaking twist: instead of being angry at the program or recognizing it was harmful, many people turn that pain inward. They blame themselves. They think they failed the program. They believe they weren't ready, weren't serious enough, weren't good enough.

The fiction becomes fact in their minds: *I'm the problem. I deserved this.*

It's a strange but very real pattern. People who get kicked out of abusive recovery programs sometimes end up going back on their own. It sounds unbelievable until you understand how deeply trauma can shape someone's sense of reality. That kind of emotional damage doesn't just fade. It rewires how you think, especially when the trauma is wrapped up in the promise of healing.

The cycle often starts the moment someone enters the program. They're promised they'll find safety, support, and a real shot at getting better. That promise feels like hope, particularly for someone who's already been through chaos or neglect. But things shift once a person is in the program. The promise of community becomes control. Vulnerability gets weaponized. Emotional breakdowns in front of the group are demanded. This exposure puts participants at risk.

The staff actually wield the power to control how participants see themselves, their recovery, and their worth. The message is clear. If you follow the rules, break yourself open, submit completely, then maybe you'll get better. This forces people to give up their autonomy in the name of healing. And they're often too emotionally entangled to just walk away once they come to understand what's really happening.

When someone gives that much of themselves to a program—when they fully buy in, follow the rules, and build their identity around the recovery process—getting kicked out can feel absolutely unbearable. It's not just rejection. It feels like total failure. By the time they're expelled, participants have often been emotionally conditioned to believe that messing up means they've let everyone down.

And then, just like that, the structure they depended on is gone. The routines, the rules, the people are suddenly cut off. This inflicts a crushing sense of isolation. Any outside support system they once had may no longer exist or may no longer feel safe. At that point, desperation kicks in. The fear of life without the program becomes too big. This leads people to return to the program. It doesn't seem to matter that they'll fall into the same dynamic of emotional control and abuse. It feels safer than being completely alone.

That kind of attachment to being controlled becomes cemented, in large part, through experiences of shame. It settles deep in your body and affects your sense of self. People are regularly pressured to confess things publicly. Then they get called out by their peers for the things they have confessed. This can include emotionally intense confrontations. These experiences are often labeled as "accountability." But this behavior crosses a line. When confessions are forced and manipulated, they break people down.

True and healthy accountability can be powerful. It can help people face tough truths and make real changes. But in programs that revolve around control rather than care, accountability turns into coercion. And shame becomes a weapon.

One former participant from a non-residential recovery program shared that she was made to stand in front of everyone while they called out her flaws. When she started crying, she was accused of being manipulative by using her tears to get sympathy. It was humiliating. Still, she kept going back. When asked why, she said something that really stuck: "At least there, I felt like someone saw me. Outside of that room, no one cared if I lived or died.[3]

That's the heartbreaking part. The more pain and isolation people feel in these programs, the more attached they often become. It's a strange, painful loyalty. Psychologically, it's not so different from what keeps people glued to slot machines or stuck in abusive relationships—what's known as *intermittent reinforcement*. You never know when you'll get a scrap of approval or attention, so you keep coming back, hoping this time will be different.[4]

I still remember the day I got kicked out and how small and worthless I felt. I thought I'd hit rock bottom, but the real collapse came after, when I begged to be let back in. I stood there, crying in front of everyone, completely exposed, and they let me back—but only after making it clear how messed up and weak I was and how much I had failed everyone. And the worst part? I believed them. I truly thought I deserved it. I thought being humiliated like that was part of my healing. So when I came back, I didn't just keep quiet. I doubled down. I tried harder to "get it right." I did my best not to question the rules. I told myself that speaking out or complaining was just proof that I wasn't ready. Looking back, I can see now how deep the shame ran, and how staying silent started to feel like the only way to survive.

Speaking up about the toxic tactics—like coercion, shame, and the fear of getting kicked out—is often seen as disloyal. People are made to feel like they're betraying the group just for telling the truth. And if you do speak out, you're quickly labeled as someone who "isn't working the program" or who "wasn't ready." That kind of thinking creates a culture of silence, one that doesn't just affect current participants but often sticks with people who go on to become staff themselves. Criticism isn't taken seriously—it's dismissed as bitterness or blamed on "dry drunk" resentment. Meanwhile, staying loyal—no matter what—is treated like a spiritual badge of honor.

Dr. Ingrid Clayton, a clinical psychologist who works with people struggling with addiction and trauma, explains that what looks like loyalty in abusive systems is often just fear in disguise. In unhealthy environments, people can confuse fear-based obedience with genuine commitment.[5] It's not that they want to stay; it's that they don't feel safe leaving.

And this silence can be deadly. When people get kicked out of programs for breaking rules—with no support, no safety net, and nowhere to go—some of them don't make it. They relapse. They overdose. They die. And their families are often left with no way to hold anyone accountable.

That's partly because many of these treatment centers are private, for-profit operations that have very little oversight. There's often no requirement for proper licensing, no real inspections, and no formal standards of care. Confidentiality laws, which are supposed to protect patients, can actually end up protecting the programs instead by allowing them to bury incident reports and avoid scrutiny when things go wrong. Even when things go deadly wrong.

ELEVEN

I'm sitting in a group therapy session. We're going around the circle doing check-ins, but I can't stop staring at what's missing. My mind is stuck on it. I hear the words people are saying, their voices blending together, but none of it's landing.

In my head, I see Patrick's whole body shake. It's the way he laughed, and he was always laughing. His laugh was loud and full, and it didn't stop at his mouth. It rolled through him like it tickled every part of his body. I close my eyes for a second, just to see it more clearly.

Over the last four months, being around him just made things easier. Lighter. Happier. Everyone felt it. He brought an ease to the group, this weird kind of joy. I remember one night, a bunch of us were standing around laughing—about what, I don't even remember. In the middle of it, Patrick leaned toward me and said, "This is great, right?"

"Yeah, man. I can't stop laughing around you."

He nodded. "It's what I live for."

"Right on."

"I'm serious," he said. "It keeps me going."

And just for a second, there was a shift. Something passed over his face—like the joy slipped and something sad broke through. It happened so fast I convinced myself I imagined it.

He never tried to be the center of anything, but we all gravitated toward him. He could be sitting alone in a corner, and still somehow end up pulling everyone in. He lifted the room without even trying.

It wasn't until later, too much later, that I started to understand what that laughter might have been holding back. It helped keep the other stuff at bay: the guilt, the fear, the anger. The counselor said he used drugs to cope with the loss of his dad. It was how he acted out the pain he didn't know what to do with.

Maybe that was true. Maybe, in a different environment, that insight could've helped him. But where we were, it felt more like a label than a lifeline. Something said in passing, when what Patrick needed was someone to really see him.

People are standing around in little clusters, talking quietly. It's the first thing I notice as I step inside the building. There's a hum of voices, but no real energy behind it—no laughter, no goofing around. Something's up.

I spot Tyler and Sam near the back wall. Both of them look more serious than usual.

"He's out, man. Patrick's gone," Tyler says as I walk up.

"Yeah, kicked out. Just like that." Sam tries to snap his fingers for emphasis, but he can't. That used to make us laugh, but right now, it just hangs in the air.

"I don't get it. Why?"

Tyler leans closer, lowering his voice. "Don't talk about it. Don't let them know we know."

"Right. I just... I don't actually *know*."

Before anything else can be said, Teddy's voice cuts through the room.

"Circle up!" His words shut everyone down. We move into a circle like we've done a hundred times.

"Quick announcement. Patrick fucked up. He's out. You know what that means. No talking about him. He's nothing to us now. Not worth our time. If you're caught reaching out, you're out on your ass. No second chances."

And just like that, he turns and walks into his office, shutting the door behind him.

Patrick's gone. I still don't know what happened.

◈

Later, I'm leaning against Tyler's car with him, parked way back in the corner of the lot where it's dark.

"So what actually happened to Patrick?"

Tyler shakes his head. "Corey, seriously, don't ask around. If word gets back that you're talking about him, it won't matter what your intentions are. They'll boot you just like that."

I nod slowly. "It's just weird, being on this side of it. Knowing what it feels like to be the one kicked out."

"Yeah," he says. "I bet it is."

"It's kind of fucked up."

He shrugs. "It is. But that's just how it works."

We let the silence settle between us, waiting for Sam.

I finally say, "At least tell me what you heard. What happened?"

"Dude! You gotta let it go." Tyler takes a quick look around and lowers his voice. "He got caught high again. They told his parents the only way he could come back was if they put him in a full-time inpatient program."

"You think they'll do it?"

"Yeah. That's what people are saying."

A loud slap on the car hood makes us both jump.

"Caught y'all!"

"Fuck it, Sam!" Tyler yells, clearly rattled. "Don't do that."

Sam grins but drops it just as fast. "Chill. Just saying it could've been someone else. Someone not so friendly."

That lands hard. And he's right. The fear tightens in my chest. In a place like this, even asking the wrong question can put a target on your back.

✦

"Where's Patrick?" My question falls into a deep well of silence.

It's been a while and for some reason the chair he used to sit in has stayed empty. No one has come in to take his place in our group session. Today I can't seem to shake my desire to know about Patrick. I want to know how he's doing. I want to know if he's coming back. So during my check-in, I drop the question at Judy's feet, fully realizing the danger I'm putting myself in.

"Where's Patrick?" I ask again. My eyes continue to focus on the single empty chair in the circle. The only empty chair in the circle. Patrick's chair. A moment passes, and I shift my gaze to Judy. I feel myself drilling down on her with my eyes. Her silence around my question unnerves the others.

Judy is the counselor. She should know something. But her silence betrays her allegiance to the rules and to her employer.

"Corey, you know the rules. We don't talk about people who were unwilling to help themselves."

The tone of her voice is steady, dominating. It allows her to reassert control. The tone of her voice dares us to react to her next words.

"Patrick took his life two nights ago. He was weak. He let us all down."

Wait! What? I scream inside my head.

Judy glares at me in a cold and clinical way, giving space for her words both to cut through me and to force me into compliance. I want to push back, but I'm too scared. I can't get kicked out again. Externally, I give all the cues to show that I'm backing down. I relax my body. I lower my eyes. I nod my head. Internally, I'm on fire with rage.

It's like the room shatters. I see it all in my mind—like stained glass breaking into sharp, glittering pieces. Everything I thought I understood about this place starts to come undone.

Judy glances around the circle, finding a new set of eyes to look at with each statement she makes. "He made a choice. He walked away from recovery. Then his family refused to follow through with treatment. And now he's gone."

By this point, I've managed enough courage to look at her, and I'm the only person looking at her as she continues, "That's the reality of what happens when you refuse to take this shit seriously."

I can't tell if the others are silent because of the shock, or their fear, or because they're following the lead of the group as a whole. A bitter, nasty taste creeps into the back of my mouth.

"Let this be a wake-up call." Judy's voice rises, trying to rally our support. "This is life or death, guys. If you're sitting here thinking

relapse is an option or thinking your parents owe you something, get it through your head now. Relapse isn't an option.
Your parents don't owe you shit. They don't. Patrick's parents
chose not to fight for him. They didn't want to make the
sacrifice financially. And he didn't fight for himself. Those are
the cold facts. It's what happens when you're weak."

Sarah probably knew Patrick best. She was always his biggest
fan. That's all I could think about as she spoke up. "He lied all
the time. I saw it. He just wasn't trying."

What was Sarah doing? Why was she throwing Patrick under
the bus? It wasn't true. But her words lit a fire in Judy. "Exactly.
You can't bullshit your way through this process. Patrick chose
death over accountability. Remember that people like Patrick
are weak and worthless."

I feel my body tense up. I feel like I'm going to get sick. She's
twisting the facts and we're all playing along. *What the fuck!*

"Corey, remember the rules. Don't waste any more time on
that loser or any loser who relapses. We expel losers like Patrick
from the program for good reason. We do it for the good of the
group."

❖

I lose myself in the woods, sitting at the edge of the lake. It's shaded
here, but the sunlight bounces off the still surface of the water and

into my face. I try not to squint. I want the light to burn into my eyes. But my reflex wins, and I shut them tight.

It's peaceful out here. The quiet feels almost unreal compared to the noise inside my head. The thoughts are loud and chaotic. *Patrick is gone. He took his own life.*

Judy didn't show any sadness. No sympathy. Just a stone-cold announcement that led into a lecture about weakness, failure, and responsibility. She blamed Patrick for not accepting help. She blamed his family for not trying hard enough. Plenty of blame to go around. And somehow, none of it landed on the staff.

The worst part? No one pushed back. Everyone nodded. Even me. And Sarah lied about him. She turned on him. Said he was never trying. Maybe she was scared. Maybe we all were. Our pain, our confusion, our grief—it was all swept aside and replaced by fear and shame. There was no space to feel anything real.

I keep seeing Patrick's face. I keep imagining myself in his place. That's what terrifies me. I've already been kicked out once. I know what it feels like to be erased. I know how cold it is out there. And I know—I *know*—if it happens again, I won't come back either. Not this time.

I press my palms into my knees and stare out across the glassy lake. A breeze moves through the trees above. Out here, the world feels honest in a way the program never has. But inside, I'm all knotted up. I can't believe how tangled I've become in all of this. This group. These people. This fear.

I lean forward, resting my elbows on my thighs and my chin on my arms. It's so beautiful out here. The quiet wraps around me as my thoughts settle into something heavier, deeper. I miss Patrick. I miss his laugh. The way his joy pulled us all in. And now, it's like I'm shutting down, one piece at a time.

Breathe, Corey. Just breathe.

TWELVE

Getting kicked out of a program is quick and clean—at least from the outside. It happens all the time in the treatment industry, like part of the system's routine. But no matter how routine it seems, it causes real disruption. In a healthy recovery setting, something that painful would be talked about and worked through. But in places where recovery is toxic, that pain just gets buried. There's no room for reflection. Just control, blame, and damage control.

I've been on the receiving end of that. I got kicked out once, and my life fell apart. The fear from that experience got stuck deep inside me. So when I got back in, I did whatever I had to do to stay in line. I was terrified of getting kicked out again. What I wasn't prepared for, though, was what it would feel like to be the one who stayed behind, watching someone else, like Patrick, get expelled.

It wrecked me.

Once Patrick was out, it was like he'd never existed. We weren't allowed to talk about him—not after he got kicked out, and definitely not after he died. And yet, there he was, in my head every day. His absence became this quiet warning. Just saying his name could get you booted, too. The fear wasn't hypothetical. It was close. Personal.

Everything in the group changed for me after that. I used to joke around, talk freely, and have real moments. But once Patrick was gone, I couldn't swim in that world anymore. The air got heavier. I started holding back, second-guessing others all the time. Grief had no place to go, so it turned inward. And we all knew if we wanted to stay, we had to play along. We had to stay quiet.

Being left behind was its own kind of trauma. Watching someone disappear and being told to pretend they never mattered messes with your head. There was no space to talk about what it meant or how we felt. Just silence. Forced compliance became the rule if you wanted to survive.

Recovery programs that operate like this sell themselves as places of healing. But when they rely on fear, shame, and expulsion, they do the opposite. Kicking someone out doesn't just hurt the person who's expelled. It ripples through everyone still there. It destabilizes the group, damages trust, and leaves people stuck between guilt and silence. The emotional impact lingers. It gets stuck in the body, and people carry it with them, long after the program ends.[1,2] Healing can't happen in a place where fear runs the show.

And one of the main ways that fear takes hold and spreads is through the constant threat of expulsion—a punishment that's treated as discipline, but often feels more like control.

In many of these programs, expulsion isn't a last resort. It's a go-to response. Instead of working with someone through a setback, they're shown the door. There's no space for struggle, no tolerance for being less-than-perfect. It's not about support or compassion; it's about sending a message: fall in line or get out. And while it's framed as accountability, it's really about control disguised as care. That kind of environment doesn't foster growth; it shuts it down.

And here's the thing: it just doesn't work. Tossing someone out for slipping up completely misses what addiction is really about. Addiction is complicated. It's tied up in trauma, emotional pain, and survival strategies. Those things don't just vanish when someone walks into treatment. When programs focus more on rule-breaking than root causes, people stop focusing on recovery and start focusing on avoiding punishment.[3]

I've seen it happen. Fear takes over. People keep their real struggles to themselves, afraid that being honest might get them kicked out. And once that fear sets in, the whole point of being there—healing, connection, growth—starts to fade. What's left is silence, shame, and people doing their best to stay in line rather than get better.[4]

That's the big difference between ethical programs and the ones that cause harm. In a good, well-run recovery environment, people have space to reclaim their lives and work through what brought them there in the first place. But when staff impose harsh or arbitrary rules, and when expulsion is used as a constant threat, the power imbalance becomes toxic. It turns recovery into something dangerous, especially for people who already carry trauma.[5]

When someone gets kicked out and no one's allowed to talk about it, the silence doesn't just hang in the air. It teaches everyone a lesson. People start holding back, swallowing their doubts, and hiding their struggles. Being real becomes risky. Over time, that fear gets under your skin. You stop trusting your gut. You stop speaking up. You start to believe your feelings aren't safe to have.

Expelling someone sends a clear message: fall in line or you're out. And that doesn't just hit the person who's gone—it changes the whole group. Suddenly everyone's guarded, careful, afraid to step out of bounds. But recovery isn't supposed to be about fear. It's supposed to be about connection, honesty, and feeling safe enough to heal. When fear takes over, all of that disappears, all that makes us human starts to disappear.

Grief is part of being human. It's normal and necessary. Whether we're dealing with the death of someone close or the sudden loss of a group member, we need space to grieve in order to heal. When Patrick was kicked out, and then when he died, it hit us hard on two levels. But we weren't allowed to talk about it. We weren't even allowed to acknowledge it. We were expected to just move on and stay silent.

Being forced into silence after someone is expelled is controlling and cruel. No one talked about what happened, and no one was allowed to ask questions or say how they felt. If you did, you'd get shut down—called out, threatened, maybe even kicked out yourself. That kind of fear takes a real toll. Over time, it makes you believe you're not allowed to feel anything at all. And in recovery, where most of us are already carrying around a lot of unprocessed pain, that's dangerous.

Recovery is supposed to help you get in touch with what you're feeling. It's supposed to help us face our feelings and learn how to deal with them. But when the feeling of grief gets pushed down and ignored, that healing process gets cut off. It messes with your head, your body, your ability to feel safe. And it leaves this empty, unspoken space in the group. It's like a wound no one's allowed to look at. When programs focus more on control and silence than on honest emotional expression, they end up doing the opposite of what they're supposed to do: they block real recovery.

They said awful things about Patrick and his family—things that, outside of that setting, would've been unthinkable. But somehow, in the context of the group and the reason we were all there, it felt even worse. It crossed a line. Patrick was our friend. He was struggling, just like the rest of us. And when they told those lies and then made it clear we weren't allowed to talk about him at all, it sent a pretty loud message. It told us that our feelings didn't matter.

That kind of emotional shutdown is incredibly isolating. You're left trying to make sense of something painful without being allowed to actually feel it or talk about it. It pushes you deeper into shame. You start to believe that grief, sadness, even anger are wrong, or worse, weak. You eventually start questioning every emotion you have. You wonder if what you're feeling is okay, or if it'll get you in trouble. That constant second-guessing takes root and starts to eat away at your ability to trust yourself.

Back in the '90s, a psychiatrist named Jonathan Shay, who worked with the VA, came up with the term *moral injury*. He was working with combat veterans at the time and used it to describe what happens when someone in a position of authority betrays what's morally right in high-stakes situations.[6] That idea really fits what happens in some recovery programs too. Moral injury shows up when you're forced to follow a system that tells you to ignore your gut, silence your emotions, and go along with things you know are wrong.

When Patrick got kicked out, we all knew it wasn't right. But we were warned not to talk about it. If we did, we would get kicked out, too. That kind of threat starts to eat away at your own internal compass. You know something's wrong, but you're stuck. Speaking up is the right thing, but it feels too dangerous. So you stay quiet, even though it goes against everything you believe. It was a kind of betrayal both to Patrick and to each of ourselves.

And that doesn't just go away. The silence starts festering inside you. You start wondering if staying quiet makes you part of the problem. You feel guilty for not standing up, and you feel ashamed for going along with it. It gets to you. You carry it, and it changes how you see yourself.

It often starts to show up as a self-loathing that is brutal and tends to run deep. It turns you against yourself, chips away at your peace of mind. It shows up when you feel like you've failed your own sense of right and wrong. For some people, that guilt leads to shutting down emotionally. They learn to keep others at a distance because the fear of being seen, judged, or exposed feels too dangerous. For others, it turns into self-sabotage (sometimes even relapse) because deep down, they don't believe they deserve to get better.

That's what happened to me. I stayed quiet while the staff tore Patrick and his family apart after he got kicked out. I didn't speak up, even though I knew what they were saying was cruel and wrong. I hated myself for going along with it. I felt the same disgust toward myself that I felt toward the staff. That kind of self-loathing doesn't just fade away—it creates a split inside you. Instead of moving forward in recovery, you start sinking into a spiral of shame and self-blame that's hard to climb out of.

That experience stayed with me. It's part of a pattern that happens to many participants when someone gets kicked out.

The important thing to remember is that someone getting kicked out is about more than just losing a friend. That alone is hard, but for many of us, it goes deeper. Watching someone get expelled can bring up old wounds such as feelings of helplessness, betrayal, abandonment.[7] A lot of people come into recovery already carrying a heavy load of unresolved pain, and something like this can crack it wide open.

It's not just that old feelings get stirred up. These feelings can actually re-traumatize you. That's the part people don't always see. When you're triggered like that, you can slip back into the same emotional patterns you came to recover from. It's like emotional quicksand. You think you're moving forward, and suddenly you're stuck—caught in fear, shame, confusion. And that kind of emotional chaos can really wreck your recovery. The program starts to feel unstable and even dangerous.

Staying silent also starts to fracture you internally. You're told not to feel certain things. Not to grieve. Not to question. So you start cutting off parts of yourself just to survive in the program. You put on a mask to fit in, and little by little, you lose touch with who you really are.

Dr. Bessel van der Kolk talks about how being forced to deny your real feelings in order to stay safe creates a kind of internal split. You feel disconnected from your own emotions, and that disconnection makes real healing almost impossible.[8]

That was definitely true for me. After Patrick was kicked out, and then especially after he died, I felt that split hard. I couldn't reconcile the part of me that cared and wanted to speak up with the part that was too scared to break the rules. I'd been kicked out before, and I knew what that meant. So I stayed quiet. But over time, that silence made me feel like a stranger to myself. I didn't know who I was anymore—not outside the program, and not even inside it. That confusion and fear sticks with you. And it teaches you to perform on cue, even when you don't feel strong enough or safe enough to.

THIRTEEN

The folding chairs squeak against the shiny linoleum floor as we settle into an uneven circle. Twenty-four of us, each somewhere on the spectrum of pain, recovery, or just trying to look like we belong. The air is stale under the harsh fluorescent lights. We all know what's about to happen. It fills the room with tension. Grow-or-Go sessions always put us on edge. Nobody wants to draw attention, but there's nowhere to hide.

Judy sits at the top of the circle. She holds herself tight and upright, like posture is power. Her smile is well-rehearsed, almost perfect. But there's an edge to it. She doesn't use it to comfort. She uses it to cut.

I cross my arms, keep my eyes low, and try to blend into the wall at my back. I just need to stay quiet. Last night wrecked me. My dad was trying to talk to me with my mom yelling from the bedroom. She was in pain and strung out on who knows what. He said he might have to pull the plug on the power. He'd try to keep the water on. He's giving up. I heard it in his voice. He'll be walking away soon enough.

And here I am. Trapped in this room full of strangers, pretending to heal.

"All right," Judy says. She is way too cheerful. "Someone in here has been dragging the energy down. You know who you are."

I don't look up, but I can feel some of the heads turn. I know my name is already on her tongue.

"Corey."

My stomach knots up. *Fuck.*

"Let's hear from you," she says.

"I'm good," I mutter.

Judy tilts her head. "I didn't ask if you were good. You've been coming in here like a ghost for weeks. It's disrespectful and a real turn-off. Either say something or stop sucking the life out of the room."

Laughter. A few snorts. I feel my face heating up.

"I don't really feel like talking right now," I say.

"You've made that clear. But that's not how this works. You either grow or you go, Corey. And right now? You're about to go."

My whole body tenses up as I feel myself shut down, but something in me manages to break free. Maybe it's lack of sleep, or the panic that's racing through me out of fear of being cornered. Maybe I am just sick of holding it all in.

"I don't think this is working." My words are tentative and quiet.

"What's not working?" she asks.

"The program."

I see people turn to look at me out of the corner of my eye.

"Why don't you tell us what's not working, since you apparently know everything?"

I exhale hard. "My dad just lost his job," I say, staring at a stain on the floor. "We're probably gonna lose our trailer, and he's about ready to cut out on us. My mom's strung out all the time and talking to the walls. She's helpless. And I'm stuck in here while everything falls apart out there."

No one says anything. The room is still. I keep going.

"I feel like garbage in here. Like I'm some piece of white trash that got thrown in with the rich kids. Everyone here has support. Families. Money. Futures. I don't have shit. I'm not getting better. I'm getting worse. I wake up every day and it takes everything I've got not to scream as I drag myself here."

My voice cracks on the last word.

"I don't belong here," I whisper.

And then my eyes blur. Tears. Fucking tears.

I look up. It's a mistake. I see everyone staring at me. Some are blank stares. Some are snickering as they look on. I feel like I'm some science experiment going wrong.

"You done?" Judy asks in a sharp tone.

"What?"

"I asked if you're done feeling sorry for yourself."

I blink, stunned. I start to open my mouth, but no sound comes out.

"Jesus Christ," she snaps. "Are you crying right now?"

Someone laughs. The guy to my right elbows the dude next to him.

"Wow." Judy pauses for dramatic effect. "I said speak your truth, not turn it into a fucking sob story. Man the fuck up, Corey. Quit acting like a little bitch."

I freeze. My whole body locks down. The word *bitch* hits harder than anything. Why can't I disappear?

"I didn't ask for this," I say, shaking. "I didn't ask for this life or these parents or any of this. I just want to go. I need to get out of this room."

"Run away?" Judy barks. "That's your solution?"

"No."

"Then work the fucking program!" Now, she's shouting.

I stare at her, hollow. "I don't know what that means. No one's ever explained it. Y'all just say that over and over like it's magic."

I feel like I'm suffocating. I can't breathe.

"You know what your problem is, Corey? You're stuck in your own head. You're addicted to your own story. You're not that special. Everyone here has trauma. You think you've got the worst story in the room? Please."

"I never said that."

"You think you're better than the rest of us. But you're not. You're white trash, Corey. That's who you are. Embrace it. Quit trying to act like you're some misunderstood genius with a tragic past. You're not. You're just another angry, broke kid who doesn't want to grow the fuck up."

I can't speak. My mouth doesn't work anymore. All I can do is sit there while the tears keep falling. My body starts to shake.

Then, all of a sudden, Judy moves on like nothing has happened. She turns and calls on someone else. Everyone shifts their attention from me to the next victim. And here I sit, alone inside this room full of people.

In the common room after the session, I lean against a wall in the corner with a cup of coffee in my hand. I'm looking at nothing in particular, still trying to get back into my body.

"Yo, Corey!" one of the guys shouts. "Need a tampon, dude?"

Laughter rolls through the room.

Another voice mocks my words: "My mom's talking to the walls and I feel like white trash—wahhhh."

The laughter seems to be louder now.

"Don't take it so seriously, Corey." Tyler walks up and puts a hand on my shoulder. "We're just trying to help you lighten up."

He leans in to give me a hug. I just stand there, fists clenched, throat raw.

A moment passes, and I look over to Tyler. "Can you give me a lift home?"

Standing in front of the trailer, I wait for the silence as Tyler's car drives away. It doesn't come though. The porch light hums above me, dull and flickering like everything else here. I see the glow of the TV against the curtains of the front window. My dad's either asleep or pretending to be. I don't look too long. If I do, I'll go in. And I can't do that.

Not tonight.

It's too small in there, and too full of things I can't deal with. I notice I'm not breathing, so I take a big breath in and let it out slowly. Part of me thinks I'm being a drama queen and wants to shut my feelings down. But I'm not going to let it happen.

Not tonight.

So I turn and walk away.

I head down the dirt road. It loops around the trailer park and winds past old junker cars and plastic lawn chairs that haven't moved in months. Everything out here is worn out and forgotten.

It's not just the stuff, either. It's the people, too. The lives around here are just as tired, just as left behind. This is the part of town you end up in when others want to forget you, when the rest of the world doesn't want to see you anymore. For whatever reason. Out of sight, out of mind.

I keep walking until the lights behind me fade.

At the edge of the lot behind the trailer park, the old church sits quiet in the dark. It looks like a good place for me right now.

The church building is burned out and falling in on itself. Its windows are gone. It's the kind of place no one pays attention to anymore. Somehow that feels like the place I need to be right now.

I just need space to stretch in the quiet, away from light and people. So I stretch out on an empty patch of warm dirt in front of what's left of the church steps.

I look up at the sky. The stars are faint behind a layer of summer haze. I just lie here and wait in the dark until the quiet stops ringing in my ears. Until I feel solid enough to stand.

Then I get up and head back toward the trailer.

The porch light is still flickering and buzzing. It's still trying to hold the dark back.

But it can't.

Not tonight.

FOURTEEN

Not everything in recovery looks the way it's supposed to. By now, you get that. One part of my experience that really stuck with me was something called "Grow or Go." That was the name for a certain type of group session we had. It was meant to challenge us, hold us accountable, and keep us moving forward. At least, that was the idea. But in practice, it felt more like a setup. A way to single someone out and put them on the spot while everyone else watched. We were told that it was about growth, but most of the time, it felt like something else entirely.

The idea sounds simple on the surface. You either "grow" by participating, being honest, and showing you're committed to the program, or you "go." But the way this rule gets twisted and weaponized inside by the industry is anything but simple.[1] These aren't your average check-in circles. They're psychological minefields. You never know who's going to be in the hot seat next. And once the counselor or staff person sets their sights on you, it's game on. For me, these sessions never ended well.

What happens during "Grow or Go" sessions isn't healing. It's theater. A performance of pain, where you're either the main act or part of the audience expected to cheer on the breakdown. And when you're in the middle of it, stripped of defenses and trying to keep your shit together, there's no one coming to save you. You're on your own. The worst part is that they frame it as help. They make it sound like tough love when it's really just control dressed up in recovery jargon.

Some programs with questionable ethics try to rebrand their "Grow or Go" sessions by giving them softer, more familiar names—like "Primary Purpose" meetings. It sounds harmless enough, right? But here's the thing: in traditional 12-step programs like AA or NA, a Primary Purpose meeting is actually a supportive space. It's about people sharing their experiences, offering mutual support, and steering clear of telling others how to live or recover.

That's not what's happening in these coercive groups. They might borrow the name, but what they're running is something entirely different. It's usually the same old high-pressure, confrontational setup—just dressed up to look like something more legitimate. It's a way to appear aligned with well-respected recovery traditions while still using the same manipulative tactics that defined those Grow or Go sessions in the first place.

There's something uniquely damaging about being in a place that promises healing and then turns that promise against you. Especially when you're a kid who already thinks you're broken. The language of recovery (words like *truth*, *growth*, and *responsibility*) gets used to shame you, silence you, and keep you in line. Looking back now, it's clear that the Grow or Go sessions didn't help me grow. They made me afraid to speak, afraid to feel, and afraid to be seen. And that fear didn't go away when I left the room. It followed me.

This part of the story tends not to get talked about enough. But it's important, because for a lot of us, the trauma didn't just happen before we got clean or before we became part of a recovery program. Sometimes, it happened while we were trying to get better. And that deserves to be named, too.[2]

A lot of Grow or Go sessions kick off with what feels like a forced confession. What does that mean? Basically, counselors or staff push you to admit your mistakes, relapses, or sometimes even things you never did. You're expected to spill everything in front of the whole group—and show some kind of emotion while you do it. It often turns into a performance, where the more dramatic you are, the better it seems to go over.[3]

It's a total catch-22. If you don't confess, they say you're lying or in denial. But if you do confess, that admission just gives them more ammo to shame you and keep you under their control.

Sometimes people end up making stuff up just to get the counselors off their backs and prove they're "working the program."[4]

This isn't unique to recovery groups either. The same kind of pressure happens in police interrogations, where people can be pushed into admitting things they didn't do. No matter where it happens, it leaves you feeling ashamed and confused. It messes with how you see yourself, and for some, that damage sticks around, making it even harder to stay clean.[5]

I've talked with a lot of folks who, like me, went through scores of Grow or Go sessions. They told me how they were accused of hiding stuff or not being honest, and after hours of that pressure, they started making things up just to stop the questioning. I even know people who confessed to things they never did. Whether the confession was forced or fake, it all ends in the same place. It all ends with feeling humiliated. For me, it pushed me further into the dynamic of hating myself.

Accountability is a word that gets bandied about a lot in the recovery world. It can actually be helpful in group therapy when it's done the right way. That means when it's done with respect and support. But in many of my Grow or Go sessions or Primary Purpose meetings, it wasn't like that at all. When someone admitted to messing up, instead of getting understanding, they got hammered with criticism from both the counselors and the rest of the group. It turned into this harsh show where you were made to feel small and embarrassed. The whole point was to break you down so they could "build you back up" to fit what the group wanted. Being called out in front of everyone wasn't just about owning up and being accountable; it was about isolating you and making an example out of you.[6]

In a good therapy group, safety and respect are the basics.[7] But in these programs inspired by Meehan, that all flipped around. The group wasn't a place to heal. It was more like a tool to control and punish. All that public shaming just added more shame, made people anxious, and left them feeling worthless. Instead of helping, it often became abusive and ended up doing real damage.[8]

My sessions felt like I was being stripped naked in front of everyone with nowhere to hide. I was forced to share things I didn't want to and just felt smaller and more alone because of it. I never felt safe or supported in those sessions. That's not what recovery should ever feel like.

I can remember how these sessions felt more like group attack therapy and less like group therapy. The attack part of the experiences was a regular part of how public shaming worked in the sessions. It wasn't just the counselors or staff coming down on you. They'd get everyone else to pile on, too. You'd be sitting there, and suddenly, it was like the whole group turned against you. People you thought were your friends were suddenly yelling, calling you out, accusing you of things. And the worst part? It was all by design. The counselors or staff set it up, gave the signal, and then just let it unfold.[9]

Supposedly, the goal was to tear down denial and force you to be honest. But let's be real. It was just psychological hazing. The idea was to break you down until you felt so helpless and exposed that you'd do or say whatever it took to get them off your back. And if you didn't play along? You risked getting kicked out.[10] That kind of pressure messes with your head fast.

None of it was healthy or helpful. Real therapy builds trust, not fear. It helps you open up, slowly and safely. It doesn't push you into a corner and let a crowd rip you apart. But in these programs, fear and control replaced empathy and support. People learned to fake it, say what the group wanted to hear, and bury everything else. That kind of experience never leads to healing. It just leads to shame, anxiety, and a lot of long-term damage.[11]

I remember someone once telling me what it was like for them. "They'd surround you," he said, "and people you trusted would start shouting. They'd be calling you a liar, saying how you controlled people. Screaming that you were a deadbeat, a failure. After a while, it all just broke you down, and you believed every single word of it. That's the whole point. They wanted you broken so you'd confess to whatever they decided was true—even if it wasn't."[12]

One of the scariest threats used in those Grow or Go sessions was the threat of being told to "go." If you weren't showing enough progress, questioned the rules, or if someone in the group ratted you out, you risked getting kicked out. And this wasn't just a slap on the wrist. It meant getting completely cut off from the group that had basically become your whole world.[13]

"Go" was the worst punishment they had. It wasn't always handed out right in front of everyone, but you always knew it was hanging over your head. If you got told to go, you were shut out. That meant that you were ignored in meetings, left out of activities, or flat-out told you didn't belong anymore. Sometimes, that meant being kicked out of the whole program.

That threat was brutal, especially because a lot of us had already been forced to cut ourselves off from family and friends. The group was all we had left. So the idea of being told to "go" was a really big deal. It kept people quiet and obedient to avoid being kicked out.[14]

I saw it happen to me. Someone in one of those sessions made stuff up. She said we were having sex, when we weren't. She felt like she had to give a good performance when she became the focus of the session. The staff didn't bother to check if it was true. Next thing I knew, I was told to "go." One day I was there, the next day I wasn't. No warning, no chance to explain myself. After that, I just shut down and did whatever it took not to get kicked out again. I also learned that in large part I was powerless.

In a healthy program, connection is about trust and support. But in Grow or Go or these co-opted Primary Purpose meetings, connection was a weapon, and being told to "go" was the stick that kept everyone in line.

Out of all the damaging tactics used in these sessions, perhaps the most cunning is emotional manipulation. The staff and leaders get really good at picking up on people's weak spots, and then they use those to keep you off balance. One minute they're praising you and making you feel like you're on the right track. The next minute, they're tearing you down. The whole back-and-forth between being on the right track and feeling crushed is exhausting.[15]

A big part of this is gaslighting. They tell you your feelings don't matter, that your memories are wrong, or that your gut instincts can't be trusted. And if you start to question what they're saying, suddenly you're "resisting" or "in denial." They twist it so that any doubt you have about what's going on isn't about how you're being treated—it's just proof that your addiction is talking. It's a way to shut you up and make you doubt yourself.[16]

One guy who spent three years in a program like this summed it up well: "One day you're the golden child, the next you're the scapegoat. You start thinking you're crazy. You can't trust your own mind anymore, so you just do whatever they say."[17]

This kind of manipulation wears you down slowly. You start questioning everything—your thoughts, your feelings, even who you are. You end up depending more and more on the group and the staff to tell you what's real. That's not recovery. That's control. And it's no surprise that a lot of people walk away from these programs feeling anxious, depressed, and totally lost.[18]

The tactics Bob Meehan came up with didn't just stay in one program or one city. In fact, as investigative reports and a quick online search show, his followers and former staff spread those same methods far and wide. They opened new programs all over the country—sometimes under different names or with a new look—but the core approach stayed the same. Cities like Houston, St. Louis, Kansas City, and Phoenix became hotspots for these Meehan-style recovery programs, mostly aimed at teens and young adults, promising enthusiastic sobriety and peer-led transformation.[19]

Journalist Maia Szalavitz, who's done a lot of digging into abuses in the teen treatment world, explains it well: Meehan's approach "spread through a kind of franchise model," where former clients and staff set up their own groups, copying those same harsh, controlling tactics.[20] At the heart of it all is the infamous "Grow or Go" group meeting, which became the centerpiece of treatment in these programs.

Survivor groups are still gathering hundreds of complaints, showing a clear pattern of abuse. Take the Enthusiastic Sobriety Abuse Alliance (ESAA), for example. They've collected over 280 complaints (64 of those just from Kansas and Missouri) and are working to get regulatory agencies involved. In 2023, KCUR reported that the group already used complaints about Arizona programs to file with the state's Department of Health Services, and they're preparing reports to take to other states, too.[21]

FIFTEEN

The beige chairs form a circle, like always. Their hard plastic seats are unforgiving. Mine sits too low for my legs and causes my knees to rise too high. I shift in the chair and try to stop fidgeting. Fidgeting brings attention to you. That kind of attention is never a good thing here. It usually gets interpreted to mean that you're not ready.

The church's parish hall smells like floor wax and weak coffee. Three crosses hang on one of the walls. A hand-painted banner proclaiming *GRACE IS A GIFT* stretches across the wall in front of me. Two long frosted windows just to the right catch the setting sunlight.

Across the circle, Amanda has just finished her speech. Her voice cracked right on cue, right where it was supposed to. Now, she's headed back to her chair, drying tears as they continue to fall down her face. All the staff nod like proud parents. I think Amanda is actually glowing. She's been chosen, and it shows.

"Let's give it up for Corey!" Nina says to keep the program moving forward. She claps first. Her smile is big, almost motherly. Everyone quickly starts to clap. Nothing at this moment feels genuine. The clapping, Nina's smile, Amanda's tears all feel performative.

I stand because I'm supposed to. My legs feel like they belong to someone else as I walk to the podium. My mouth stretches into a forced smile. My hands are shaking. I take a deep breath to try to steady them. Then I take another couple of deep breaths as I scan the faces in the circle. Things start to go slo-mo for a moment as I see friends I've gotten high with, friends I've disrupted the peace with, and other people I learned were not my friends. They get grouped in my mind with the staff. They've betrayed me, and I know I can't trust them.

Finally, I check my smile again, and then clear my throat.

"I, um..."

My voice sounds far away, like it's coming through the frosted glass behind me.

"Y'all know me. I was messed up and lost when I came here. I manipulated people. I hurt my family. I hurt some of you, too. I wanted the pain in me to stop. I said I wanted to change my life. The thing is, and y'all know this, I really didn't want to change. And thanks to this program, I did change. It broke me down and built me back up."

Each sentence I say falls flat in my mind. I have memorized the words. I'm repeating them now. I don't believe them.

"The program saved my life."

That's the one line that we all learn at some point. We know that it's the line that gets the nods. And true to form, just like that and on cue, the applause starts. I look around and want to laugh.

Then I turn to look at the staff. I'm hoping to see something from them. Some kind of hint. A nod. A glance. Something that conveys to me the message that I've got what it takes to stay on and become a staff member. I hate that I want it, but I do. If they pick me, I'll know that I did something right. I'll know that I'm good enough to be one of them, and that all the pain and abuse meant something.

Nina has already moved on. She looks at her clipboard and gets ready to call the next person up to speak.

Teddy told me one time that I had potential. He said that I had *the look*. I guess that, based on what I'm feeling now, I believed him. Like maybe, because I had the look, I wouldn't have to leave, and I could finally belong long term.

Reality has come home to roost and punched me in the gut. I'm not like Amanda. I feel like crying because I can't seem to outrun the fact that I'm a failure. I walk back to my chair, and Tyler squeezes my shoulder. I smile and nod out of habit, but inside, I'm hating on myself.

As the applause dies down and we all sit to listen to Sam, thoughts rapidly start to land in my mind. *Part of you wants this. You want them. You want the clipboard and the keys and the authority. All of that will mean you're safe and that you're accepted.*

Then I hear from somewhere in my heart the truth trying to break through. *This place didn't save you. It taught you to disappear.*

I glance down at the certificate in my hands. It reads *Graduate,* but that means nothing. I dropped out of school because they told me I had to in order to focus on healing. My mother is still a drug addict. My father is even more MIA than ever. I have no friends outside of people here, and most of them aren't even close to being real friends.

Sam finishes up to a round of applause and smiles. I watch as he makes his way back to his seat. As the clapping dies down and before Nina can call the next person, I feel a low voice breathe words in my direction. "Do they make you say it like that?"

I turn my head slightly to my left to look at Marcus. He's a new kid, maybe sixteen. Our eyes meet for a split-second. I see me in them, and I hear me in his question.

Nina clears her throat. I wasn't the only one to hear Marcus's question. She cuts a look in my direction as she calls out for the next person to come forward. Someone claps to smooth the awkward pause, and the ritual moves on.

But with Marcus's question, something breaks through inside of me. If he can actually see me for me, then I'm not all lost. I'm not all fucked up. Maybe I do matter.

After two months of AA meetings in this dingy church basement, I'm noticing that it always smells the same. It's damp wood and years and years of old coffee. The fluorescent lights above me buzz and flicker. They so want to give up and short out. I can relate. Their low electric hum flows through my head. The folding chairs make uneven rows, laid out too close together.

I'm sitting near the corner of the room, trying to disappear. If I stay still enough, maybe no one will ask anything. My hands are shaking and my legs are restless. I clench my hands into fists and push them into my lap. It's the only way I know to feel at least a little grounded.

After these two months, it still feels like I'm crashing someone else's party. The people here talk about wives and kids, long shifts at work, the ways their faith pulled them through. I can't relate to any of it. They talk about missing Christmas with their families. All I can think is how that doesn't seem like a big deal to me. I missed high school. I missed normal life.

Every time someone finishes speaking, I feel myself tensing up. My story isn't neat or clean. It's all raw edges, ups and downs, missing pieces, abuse, and trauma. I don't want to share, so when I finally force something out, it's only a few sentences. Then I shut down.

The phrase *one day at a time* is thrown around in every meeting like it's supposed to solve something. But to me, it feels like a riddle I can't crack. I still haven't gotten around to understanding what the hell a day means without having the group's schedule telling me what to do, when to do it, and who to hang around.

And then there's the word *sponsor*. Everyone keeps saying it like it's Jesus Christ's job description. They profess how it's the person who keeps them pulled together when everything else falls apart. I don't know how to ask for something like that. I'm not sure I even know how to be someone worth helping.

As the meeting comes to a close and people start to mill around and head out, I bend over and pretend to tie my shoe. I find it's a good way to avoid these people. As my eyes are focused on my shoelace, I see another pair of shoes walk into frame. I look up to see a portly older man smiling down at me. He moves slowly as he starts to sit in the chair next to me. I bolt up.

"Hey, Corey," he says, quiet and calm, with eyes that don't search me for anything. "I'm Jim. I've seen you here a few times now."

I nod a little as my body tenses up. I heard in the group how AA is filled with old gay guys, so now I'm waiting to get hit on. I'm also waiting for the part where he says I'm doing it wrong.

He offers his hand and says, "It's hard. But you're showing up. That counts."

I don't know what to say. I feel cornered and forced to shake his hand. Words get jammed somewhere in my throat.

"If you ever want to talk," he says, "I can sponsor you. No pressure. Just someone to check in with, when you need it."

The word *sponsor* lands heavy in my chest, but not in a scary or oppressive way. This time it sounds and feels different. It sounds like an invitation to explore. Then I notice how I'm feeling more relaxed. Something about Jim's voice and the calm he embodies puts me at ease.

"Maybe." It's all I can manage.

Jim nods like that's enough. Then he pulls out a card from his pocket and hands it to me. It's a business card with his name and number.

"No rush," he says. "Just remember you're not alone."

I stare down at the card and let his words settle around me. He gets it. I feel fucking alone. But with his few words, I begin to feel seen. It's such a small interaction, but it's a start. And for the first time in what feels like years, I feel something stir. I feel something small and almost weightless. Not joy. Not even hope, really. Just a little room to breathe.

✦

My eyes drift to take in the scene. The summer heat is fading, and leaves are starting to change. The light is shifting and softening, too. A mix of people are sitting at some of the other outside tables enjoying the tamer afternoon sun. I hear the low, quiet hum of conversation drifting between tables. No particular conversation draws me into it like I want it to. No particular person distracts me from myself like I want someone to. So I come back to where I'm sitting, across from Jim, with my hands wrapped around a cup of coffee that I haven't touched. It's too hot, but I keep holding it like it'll keep me from running away.

Jim doesn't rush. He just watches me with that steady calm that I've come to appreciate. With it, he lets me know that he's not here to fix me. He's just here while I find my way through this mine field.

"Getting your GED is the first step," he says matter-of-factly. "School's not just about books and tests. It's a way into something real. It may sound trite, but it's a way to make a fresh start for yourself.

I nod slowly and unsure. "I dropped out. I didn't finish any-thing." I start to feel overwhelmed. "I don't even know where to begin."

Jim doesn't flinch. "That's okay. Nobody expects you to have it all figured out. You just need one place to start. One real step."

"This town," my voice starts to crack. "It's a trap. I'll always be white trash here. I've got to find a way to get away, so I can be me."

Jim leans in. He speaks in a relaxed, grounded voice. "I hear you. But the only way to truly get away is to stop running away."

He sees the look of confusion on my face.

"Running away keeps you spinning in circles. It keeps kicking you down. But go back to school and you train your mind to carry you further than your past and your mistakes ever did. No one can take that from you."

I look away. There's a knot in my throat I can't quite speak through. But something starts to stir inside me. Some kind of tension starts to break up.

"Think of it this way, Corey. Education doesn't just open doors. It builds roads and paths forward. That's how you make sure that when you leave you're not running away from some-thing but you're heading somewhere that you choose.

"I don't know if I can pull it off."

Jim nods. "It won't be easy."

I don't say anything. I just sit in between being scared and feeling hopeful that what he's telling me is true.

"If you want to get away, build yourself up and climb out, don't beat yourself up and disappear."

SIXTEEN

Graduation from The Group is supposed to be a big deal. A time to look back on everything you've worked through and a time to look forward to what's next. It's meant to feel like a turning point—hopeful, exciting, full of possibility. Mine had all the surface stuff: people, clapping, a few heartfelt speeches, staff saying how proud they were. But the truth? It felt hollow. Just another performance. I knew exactly what to say and how to say it. I'd learned that part well. Smile, thank everyone, act inspired. Inside, I felt like I was playing a part in someone else's script.

The whole thing was just for show. They handed me a certificate, told me I'd made it. But "graduating" didn't mean I was prepared for anything. It meant I'd figured out how to stay in line long enough to get out. A lot of us stepped out into the world with no idea how to actually live in it. We'd spent years being told what to think, how to feel, when to speak. Then suddenly we were on our own, expected to manage jobs, relationships, bills, everything. No support, no real tools. Just the pressure to prove we were fixed.

I got lucky. I won't pretend otherwise. It was timing, ex-haustion, maybe a little stubbornness—just enough to push me in the right direction. But I had no roadmap. No plan. The odds weren't in my favor. I was carrying around so much damage from the program, from the way we were treated and torn down, that even thinking about a future felt like a stretch.

A lot of people don't land on their feet. They fall hard. You leave the program thinking you're healed, but then the old stuff creeps back in. The same pain, the same patterns. And now, you're supposed to just figure it out. Rebuild everything. Be better. It's overwhelming. Graduation doesn't feel like free-dom. It feels like standing at the edge of something way too big, hoping you don't fall apart.[1]

My graduation from the program looked pretty normal—for that kind of place, anyway. What I mean is, these ceremonies tend to be more about performance than anything real. You're expected to smile, to act grateful, to play the part of someone who's been transformed. The message is that you're reborn, cured, ready to take on the world. But under all the applause and staged emotions, it felt hollow. I was just trying to get through it.

And it isn't just a sendoff. It's a test. If you're tapped to join staff, you're seen as a success story, a win winner. The program holds you up as proof that their system works. And if you're not tapped to join staff? That's public. Everyone sees it. You're left standing there, feeling like you failed the final exam.

It's sick. Because by that point, the group has become your whole world. You've been cut off from your family, your friends. The people in that room are the only ones left, and now you're not good enough for them either. That sense of rejection hits hard. It's not just "you didn't make staff." It feels like "you don't belong anymore."

One graduate I talked to put it like this: "You start to believe that you're nothing without the group. They teach you not to trust yourself, so you end up depending on them to tell you who you are. And if they don't choose you, it feels like you don't exist anymore."[2]

And that's the trap. You've been told over and over again that staying sober depends on being in the group, on becoming staff, on proving yourself. And then you're not chosen. That kind of rejection doesn't just sting; it can feel like a death sentence. The fear of failing outside the program is so deeply planted that people cling to whatever hope they can, even when it's built on manipulation and fear.

Some people never recover from that moment. The shame of not being picked, of being told—implicitly or directly—that you don't measure up, can haunt you for years. That evening, for a lot of us, wasn't a celebration. It was a quiet unraveling.

One of the biggest things no one really talks about after graduation is how unprepared you are for real life. These programs, especially the Meehan-style ones, run your life for you. Every hour of your day is mapped out. You're told when to eat, what chores to do, who you can talk to, what to say—everything. There's no room to figure out how to manage life on your own, because making your own decisions is treated like a threat to your recovery.

So when the program ends, you're suddenly dropped into the real world with zero experience making choices for yourself. You don't know how to do the basics. I'm talking about cooking a meal, taking the bus, paying a bill, and applying for a job. Some people didn't even know how to make a doctor's appointment. These things might seem small, but they're not—especially when no one's ever let you try before. Worse, in those programs, showing any kind of independence was usually punished, not encouraged. It was safer to stay dependent.

That kind of environment creates a learned helplessness. It trains you to look to authority for every answer, and when you don't have that anymore, you freeze. Research backs this up. People who come out of rigid recovery programs without life skills training are more likely to relapse or wind up unemployed, even homeless.[3] That should shock you, but not surprise you. A person needs confidence and basic tools to get by, and without them, everything feels impossible.

I remember thinking I was ready. I wanted to be. But then I tried to fill out a job application and couldn't get past the first few questions. I didn't know where to start. That moment hit hard. It was like the whole time I thought I was being prepared for the world, I was really just being trained to survive *inside* the program. Once I was out, it felt like I was set up to fail, particularly since I didn't finish high school.

A lot of people graduate from these programs without a diploma. No GED, no high school credits, nothing to show for the months or years they spent inside the program. College? Forget it. Some never even make it back to a regular classroom.

That's not by accident. Programs modeled after Meehan's system often tell young people that school is a problem. I lived it. They said it was a "trigger," that being in school would mess with your recovery. So instead of helping you stay connected to your education, they push you to drop out completely.[4] No more teachers, no more classmates, no more outside contact. It was isolation, plain and simple, dressed up as treatment.[5]

That kind of thinking does real damage. It doesn't just pause your future. It puts a wall between you and it. You stop learning, you stop developing socially, and you lose a big part of what helps kids grow into functioning adults. Experts have been saying this for years: forcing kids out of school, puts them at higher risk of unemployment, poverty, and relapse down the line.[6]

And it's not like you can just pick up where you left off. Most employers want to see some proof you can show up, learn something, and stick with it. But when your resume has no diploma, and just a recovery program with a bad reputation, good luck getting a second look. People judge. And addiction carries its own weight of stigma that's hard to shake.

Even if you do get a job, it's usually something unstable and low-paying. That kind of work makes it hard to stay on your feet. You live paycheck to paycheck, stress piles up, and before long, you're back in the same patterns you fought so hard to break. That's why recovery programs should include real education and job training.[7] Without those, they're not really giving people a way forward. They're just sending them out unprepared and hoping for the best—and all without a human safety net.

From the start, programs like these work to cut people off from their families and friends. It's not subtle. Parents are called toxic or enabling. Longtime friends are labeled as dangerous influences. I was told to drop anyone from my life who wasn't in the program. And I did. Most of us did. It's framed as part of the healing process, but really, it's about control. The more isolated we were, the easier we were to manage.

The thing is, isolation like that doesn't set you up for success when you leave. It leaves you unsteady and alone at exactly the moment you need support the most. The research I've come across says family support is one of the biggest predictors of staying sober. Not control, not obedience—connection. Real, personal connection.[8]

But the way these programs operate destroys those connections. Families are hurt. Some feel blamed or shut out. Over time, ties break. And when it's finally over, and you step back into your old life, those relationships aren't always there to catch you. The damage has been done.

And the distrust goes beyond family. These programs teach you that the outside world is unsafe, that only the group understands you. So even if you want to reconnect, you're not sure how. You've spent so long second-guessing yourself, checking in with the group before you make a move, that when you leave, you're not sure how to think for yourself. You're trained to depend on the group—on their approval, their rules, their version of reality.[9]

That kind of thinking sticks. I remember not knowing how to talk to people once I was out. I didn't know what to say to people I had cut off. I didn't feel close to anyone outside the program. And the worst part was, I didn't trust myself enough to rebuild those connections.

These programs create a kind of emotional vacuum. Once you're out, you feel like you're floating—disconnected from everything and everyone. And without a support system to land in, that feeling of being untethered becomes dangerous. It's no wonder so many people relapse. It's not weakness. It's what happens when you leave a place that's isolated you from the people who could've helped you find your footing.

After the completion of the program, graduates are often told to go to recovery meetings, usually something like Alcoholics Anonymous (AA). That might seem like a solid next step, but for a lot of young people coming out of coercion-based programs, it's not that simple. You have to remember that these programs are strict, top-down, and controlling. Everything is decided for you: what you do, when you do it, how you feel about it. Then, suddenly, you're supposed to show up to AA, which is totally different. It's peer-led. There's no authority figure running the show, and no one's forcing you to be there.[10] For someone just leaving a rigid system, that shift can be disorienting.

Even though AA is peer-led and way less controlling than the coercive programs many people are coming out of, some meetings can still feel pretty intense. There are groups that really stick to a strict version of the 12 steps, where sponsors act like gatekeepers and messing up is treated like a moral failure instead of part of the process. In those groups, people are expected to share everything, follow unspoken rules, and fall in line—or risk being called out. For some folks, that kind of structure feels comforting. But for a lot of others—especially those just leaving top-down, coercive programs—it can feel like more of the same, just dressed up differently. Plenty of people have said they walked away because it felt too harsh or too rigid.[11] And even beyond that, recovery isn't one-size-fits-all. Most people with alcohol issues relapse at some point—studies show it's between 60 to 80% or higher—so it makes sense that strict systems don't work for everyone.[12] When the focus shifts too much toward rule-following and approval from the group, it can get in the way of actually healing.

Most of the graduates from coercive programs haven't had much practice making decisions for themselves. They're used to asking for permission or following orders, so when they walk into a room where nobody's telling them what to do, it can feel like they've lost the only structure they knew. And the day-to-day of life doesn't help. Trying to find a job, getting around without a car, figuring out where to live or how to pay bills. All of it adds up fast. That pressure, mixed with a feeling of not fitting in, makes it easy to feel lost.

The age gap only adds to the problem. In many coercion-based programs, everything is centered around peers. You're living, talking, dating, and recovering with people your own age. It's all about the group. Then you walk into a typical AA meeting and suddenly you're surrounded by people in their 40s, 50s, or older. Their lives look nothing like yours. They're talking about marriages, divorces, raising kids, or decades of drinking. It's hard to relate.[13]

A lot of young people say they miss the energy and connection from their group. For better or worse, that group was their world. There were constant hangouts, social events, this shared sense of identity. Once that's gone, and you're sitting in a room of strangers, it's easy to feel like you don't belong anywhere.

That sense of disconnection is what pushes a lot of people to stop going to programs like AA. They don't feel seen. They don't feel understood. And without that community they were so dependent on, it becomes harder to stay sober. The truth is, coercion-based programs don't prepare people to live in the real world or to find their footing in a different kind of recovery community. And when you're tossed into that world without support, even something as well known as AA can feel like just another place you don't fit in.[14]

At graduation, the message from the program is clear: you're healed. And the pressure that comes with that message is intense. You're sent out into the world with this idea hanging over your head that you should have it all figured out. And when you hit a wall (and most of us did), you start to think it's your fault. Can't keep a job? Struggling in relationships? Having doubts or falling back into old habits? The program trains you to see those things not as normal bumps in the road, but it's proof that you failed. That you didn't try hard enough. That you're still broken.

What are you supposed to do with that?

Graduates get caught up in the impossible loop of trying to live up to a version of themselves that never really existed. That's not recovery. It's trauma resulting from abuse that's been wrapped up in a fake smile. It's the fall-out from selling sanity. And it eats people alive. It kills.

Notes

Introduction

[1] Jared Kaltwasser, "Mental Health Fraud Exacts High Human and Financial Costs," *The American Journal of Managed Care*, April 21, 2023, https://www.ajmc.com/view/mental-health-fraud-exacts-high-human-and-financial-costs.

[2] American Association for Justice. "Troubled Teen Industry Abuse Litigation Group." *American Association for Justice,* https://www.justice.org/member-groups/litigation-groups/troubled-teen-industry-abuse-litigation-group#:~:text=Troubled%20Teen%20Industry%20Abuse%20Litigation,wilderness%20camps%2C%20and%20parent%20corporations.

Chapter 4

[1] Daniel Kolitz, "The Love Bomb," *The Atavist Magazine*, no. 117 (July 2021), https://magazine.atavist.com/the-love-bomb-enthusiastic-sobriety-bob-meehan-abuse-cult-drugs-rehab/.

[2] Lawrence M. Weintraub et al., "Admission Practices and Cost of Care for Opioid Use Disorder at Residential Addiction Treatment Programs in the U.S.," *Journal of Addiction Medicine*, May/June 2022, https://www.ncbi.nlm.nih.gov/pmc/articles/PMC8638362/.

[3] Unsilenced, "10 Things You Should Know About the Troubled Teen Industry," Unsilenced, https://www.unsilenced.org/10-things-you-should-know-about-the-troubled-teen-industry/.

[4] "Into the Woods: The Troubled-Teen Industry & How It Targets the Wealthy, Explained," *Town & Country, June 2023,* https://www.townandcountrymag.com/society/money-and-power/a61678972/troubled-teen-industry-explained/

[5] Partnership to End Addiction, "My Son Is Caught in the Cycle of Patient Brokering," https://drugfree.org/parent-blog/my-son-is-caught-in-the-cycle-of-patient-brokering/.

[6] U.S. Department of Health and Human Services, Office of Inspector General, "Fraud and Abuse Laws: An Overview," https://oig.hhs.gov/compliance/physician-education/fraud-abuse-laws/.

[7] CBS News, "Some Addiction Treatment Centers Turn Big Profits by Scaling Back Care," https://www.cbsnews.com/news/drug-treatment-rehab-private-equity-profits/.

Chapter 6

[1] National Association of Addiction Treatment Providers, *NAATP Code of Ethics*, 2023, https://www.naatp.org/programs /ethics/code-ethics.

[2] Substance Abuse and Mental Health Services Administration. *SAMHSA's Concept of Trauma and Guidance for a Trauma-Informed Approach*. (HHS Publication No. SMA 14-4884)(Rockville, MD: Substance Abuse and Mental Health Services Administration, 2014.), https://library.samhsa.gov/sites /default/files/sma14-4884.pdf

[3] Shoshana Walter, "American Rehab," *Reveal* from The Center for Investigative Reporting, 2019, https://revealnews.org/americ an-rehab.

[4] This quote was reported to the author by Jane Doe 1 and aligns with numerous firsthand accounts from residential recovery program survivors. For a collection of similar testimonies, see *"Our Stories,"* BCS Network, https://bcsnetwork.org/category/our-st ories/.

[5] American Addiction Centers, "Communicating with a Loved One in Rehab," https://americanaddictioncenters.org/rehab-gui de/communicating-with-loved-one-in-rehab.

[6] William L. White, "The Lessons of Language: Historical Perspectives on the Rhetoric of Addiction," *Journal of Substance Abuse Treatment* 12, no. 2 (1995): 77–87.

Chapter 8

[1] Gabor Maté, "Emptiness and the Hunger for Love," in *In the Realm of Hungry Ghosts: Close Encounters with Addiction* (Toronto: Knopf Canada, 2010), 295–312.

[2] Albert Bandura, *Social Learning Theory* (Englewood Cliffs, NJ: Prentice Hall, 1977).

[3] Tamara Beetham, Brendan Saloner, Mawuli Gaye, Sarah E. Wakeman, Richard G. Frank, and Benjamin P. Linas, "Admission Practices and Cost of Care for Opioid Use Disorder at Residential Addiction Treatment Programs in the US," *Health Affairs* 40, no. 2 (2021): 317–325, https://www.ncbi.nlm.nih.gov/pmc/articles/PMC8638362.

[4] Steven C. Hayes, *Acceptance and Commitment Therapy: The Process and Practice of Mindful Change* (New York: The Guilford Press, 2004).

[5] Evelyn Tsisin, "The Troubled Teen Industry's Troubling Lack of Oversight," *The Regulatory Review*, June 27, 2023, https://www.theregreview.org/2023/06/27/tsisin-the-troubled-teen-industrys-troubling-lack-of-oversight/

Chapter 10

[1] Jennifer J. Freyd, *Betrayal Trauma: The Logic of Forgetting Abuse* (Cambridge, MA: Harvard University Press, 1996).

[2] Bessel A. van der Kolk, *The Body Keeps the Score: Brain, Mind, and Body in the Healing of Trauma* (New York: Penguin Books, 2014).

[3] Interview with Jane Doe 2, survivor of a non-residential recovery program who requested to remain anonymous.

[4] Martin E. P. Seligman, *Helplessness: On Depression, Development, and Death* (San Francisco: W.H. Freeman, 1975).

[5] Ingrid Clayton, "What Is Trauma-Bonding?" *Psychology Today*, September 16, 2021, https://www.psychologytoday.com/us/blog/emotional-sobriety/202109/what-is-trauma-bonding.

Chapter 12

[1] William L. White, Christy K. Scott, Michael L. Dennis, and Michael G. Boyle, "It's Time to Stop Kicking People Out of Addiction Treatment," *Counselor* (Deerfield Beach) 6, no. 2 (April 2005): 12–25, https://www.ncbi.nlm.nih.gov/pmc/articles/PMC6338434/.

[2] Lucy Williamson, "Creating an Ethical Culture to Support Recovery from Substance Use Disorders," *Journal of Medical Ethics* 47, no. 12 (2021): e9, https://jme.bmj.com/content/47/12/e9.

[3] William R. Miller and Stephen Rollnick, *Motivational Interviewing: Helping People Change*, 3rd ed. (New York: Guilford Press, 2013).

[4] "Expanding the Continuum of Substance Use Disorder Treatment," *Frontiers in Psychiatry* 12 (2021): Article 785996. https://www.ncbi.nlm.nih.gov/pmc/articles/PMC8815796/.

[5] G. Alan Marlatt and Dennis M. Donovan, eds., *Relapse Prevention: Maintenance Strategies in the Treatment of Addictive Behaviors*, 2nd ed. (New York: Guilford Press, 2005).

[6] Jonathan Shay, *Achilles in Vietnam: Combat Trauma and the Undoing of Character* (New York: Scribner, 1994), 20–21. The concept has since been applied to other contexts where individuals are forced to suppress their moral instincts and comply with harmful systems. See, for example, Wendy Dean and Simon Talbot, "Physicians Aren't 'Burning Out.' They're Suffering from Moral Injury," *STAT* (July 26, 2018), https://www.statnews.com/2018/07/26/physicians-not-burning-out-they-are-suffering-moral-injury/.

[7] Jessica Van Denend, J. Irene Harris, Brian Fuehrlein, and Ellen L. Edens, "Moral Injury in the Context of Substance Use Disorders: A Narrative Review," *Current Treatment Options in Psychiatry* 9, no. 4 (2022): 321–330, https://www.ncbi.nlm.nih.gov/pmc/articles/PMC9483387/.

[8] Bessel A. van der Kolk, *The Body Keeps the Score: Brain, Mind, and Body in the Healing of Trauma* (New York: Viking, 2014).

Chapter 14

[1] Sarah Beller, "The Love Bomb," *The Atavist Magazine*, https://magazine.atavist.com/the-love-bomb.

[2] Maia Szalavitz, *Help at Any Cost: How the Troubled-Teen Industry Cons Parents and Hurts Kids* (New York: Riverhead Books, 2006).

[3] Maia Szalavitz, *Help at Any Cost: How the Troubled-Teen Industry Cons Parents and Hurts Kids* (New York: Riverhead Books, 2006).

[4] Michael Welner, Matt DeLisi, and Taylor Janusewski, "False Confessions: An Integrative Review of the Phenomenon," *Behavioral Sciences & the Law* 43, no. 2 (March–April 2025): 185–202, https://doi.org/10.1002/bsl.2707.

[5] Saul M. Kassin, "False Confessions: Causes, Consequences, and Implications for Reform," *Policy Insights from the Behavioral and Brain Sciences* 1, no. 1 (2014): 112–21, https://web.williams.edu/Psychology/Faculty/Kassin/files/Kassin%20(2014)%20-%20PIBBS%20review.pdf.

[6] Szalavitz, *Help at Any Cost.*

[7] Mental Health Academy, "Ethical Considerations in Group Therapy," https://www.mentalhealthacademy.com.au/blog/ethical-considerations-in-group-therapy.

[8] Beller, "The Love Bomb."

[9] William L. White, "Attack Therapy," in *Slaying the Dragon: The History of Addiction Treatment and Recovery in America*, 2nd ed. (Bloomington, IL: Chestnut Health Systems, 2014).

[10] Szalavitz, *Help at Any Cost.*

[11] I. D. Yalom and M. A. Lieberman, "A Study of Encounter Group Casualties," *Archives of General Psychiatry* 25, no. 1 (1971): 16–30, https://doi.org/10.1001/archpsyc.1971.01750130018002.

[12] Personal conversation with John Doe, former program participant who requested to remain anonymous.

[13] Enthusiastic Sobriety Abuse Alliance, "Enthusiastic Sobriety: 101," Enthusiastic Sobriety Abuse Alliance, March 1, 2018, https://www.esaalliance.org/enthusiastic-sobriety-101.

[14] Enthusiastic Sobriety Abuse Alliance, "Enthusiastic Sobriety: 101."

[15] Szalavitz, *Help at Any Cost.*

[16] Enthusiastic Sobriety Abuse Alliance, "Gaslighting and The Group," Enthusiastic Sobriety Abuse Alliance, https://www.esaalliance.org/blog/gaslighting-and-the-group.

[17] Enthusiastic Sobriety Abuse Alliance, "Gaslighting and The Group."

[18] Szalavitz, *Help at Any Cost.*

[19] Beller, "The Love Bomb."

[20] Szalavitz, *Help at Any Cost.*

[21] Noah Taborda, "Former Members Allege Reckless and Isolating Behavior at Kansas City Teenage Addiction Program," *KCUR 89.3,* February 22, 2023, https://www.kcur.org/health/2023-02-22/former-members-alle

ge-reckless-and-cult-behavior-at-kansas-city-teenage-addiction-pr
ogram .

Chapter 16

[1] Alexandre B. Laudet and William L. White, "Recovery Capital as Prospective Predictor of Sustained Recovery, Life Satisfaction, and Stress Among Former Poly-Substance Users," *Substance Use & Misuse* 43, no. 1 (2008): 27–54, https://doi.org/10.1080/108 26080701681473.

[2] Personal conversation with Jane Doe 3, former program participant who requested to remain anonymous.

[3] Daisy Gómez, Leonard A. Jason, Richard Contreras, Julia DiGangi, and Joseph R. Ferrari, "Vocational Training and Employment Attainment among Substance Abuse Recovering Individuals within a Communal Living Environment," *Therapeutic Communities* 35, no. 2 (2014): 42–47, https://www.ncbi.nlm.nih.gov/pmc/articles/PMC4089100/.

[4] Maia Szalavitz, *Help at Any Cost: How the Troubled-Teen Industry Cons Parents and Hurts Kids* (New York: Riverhead Books, 2006).

[5] Anne M. Fletcher, *Inside Rehab: The Surprising Truth About Addiction Treatment—and How to Get Help That Works* (New York: Viking, 2013).

[6] Naomi Breslau, Elizabeth Miller, Ronald C. Johnson, Pamela Lucia, Glorisa Canino, and Margarita H. Duarte, "The Impact

of Early School Behavior and Educational Achievement on Adult Drug Use Disorders: A Longitudinal Study," *American Journal of Drug and Alcohol Abuse* 34, no. 4 (2008): 465–473, https://www.ncbi.nlm.nih.gov/pmc/articles/PMC2393553.

[7] Michael R. Frone, Casey Chosewood, John C. Osborne, and John J. Howard, "Workplace Supported Recovery from Substance Use Disorders: Defining the Construct, Developing a Model, and Proposing an Agenda for Future Research," *Occupational Health Science* 6, no. 4 (2022): 475–511, https://www.ncbi.nlm.nih.gov/pmc/articles/PMC10193449.

[8] Emily A. Hennessy, Emily E. Tanner-Smith, Andrew J. Finch, Nila Sathe, and Shannon Kugley, "Recovery Schools for Improving Behavioral and Academic Outcomes among Students in Recovery from Substance Use Disorders: A Systematic Review," *Campbell Systematic Reviews* 14, no. 1 (2018): 1–84, https://doi.org/10.4073/csr.2018.9.

[9] Maia Szalavitz, *Help at Any Cost: How the Troubled-Teen Industry Cons Parents and Hurts Kids* (New York: Riverhead Books, 2006).

[10] Alcoholics Anonymous World Services, *Alcoholics Anonymous: The Big Book*, 4th ed. (New York: Alcoholics Anonymous World Services, 2001).

[11] Hannah S. Glassman, Paul Rhodes, and Niels Buus, "Exiting Alcoholics Anonymous Disappointed: A Qualitative Analysis of

the Experiences of Ex-Members of AA," *Health: An Interdiscipli-nary Journal for the Social Study of Health, Illness and Medicine* 26, no. 4 (2022): 411–30, https://pubmed.ncbi.nlm.nih.gov/32 993383.

[12] George E. Vaillant, *The Natural History of Alcoholism Revisited* (Cambridge, MA: Harvard University Press, 1995).

[13] John F. Kelly and Julie Yeterian, "Recovery Supports for Young People: What Do Existing Data Tell Us?" *New Directions for Child and Adolescent Development* 2011, no. 133 (2011): 96, https://recoveryschools.org/wp-content/uploads/2016/02/Recovery-Supports-for-Young-People.pdf.

[14] Szalavitz, *Help at Any Cost*.

Selling Sanity: Part 2

Fire

So here I am, sitting alone in this over-the-top office. It feels like a bit of a power move—make sure I have time to take in the opulence and conclude how important the guy soon to be behind the desk must be. I settle into the chair across from it. The chair's just a bit too wide, like it's designed to make you feel smaller without you even realizing it. The whole place is sleek and modern, full of chrome edges and glass. It tries a little too hard to show success. There's a bronze sculpture on the side table—maybe a wave, maybe a wing. Whatever it is, it's definitely part of the show.

I pull on the sleeve of my suit to smooth it out. The fit is perfect. It's sharp and crisp. I look like I belong here. I look like someone who's invited in through the front door and handed an espresso before the meeting starts.

No one here knows me for me. A structured jacket offers a kind of armor. It gives confidence and hides a lot. I carry myself with ease, hold steady eye contact, smile like I mean it.

But inside, it's different. There's a familiar tension, an old tug of war playing out just beneath the surface. My jaw is tight. My hands are locked in place, but I keep noticing my wrist pressing into the watch strap. *I'm so fucking skinny.*

My past still holds sway over my thoughts. The echo of being a kid trapped in a place where fear was used to discipline and where survival meant being silent and trying to go unnoticed.

The door opens.

Dr. Jordan Fields steps in with practiced ease. I size him up immediately. He's the kind of man who expects every room to carry his name. His hair is jet black, maybe a little too black. His skin is tan and definitely stretched a little too tightly across his face. His suit is darker than mine, more expensive. I have to admit that I like it.

He crosses the room like he's performing. Kind of part CEO and part motivational speaker. He extends a hand. I stand and meet it with steady confidence.

"Welcome to The Fields Treatment Center," he says, giving off an odd mix of greeting and brand pitch.

"Thanks for having me," I reply, meaning it, though not in the way he thinks.

His handshake is strong but measured, the kind you learn from highly paid consultants.

We both sit.

He picks up my résumé and scans the top like he already knows what it says. Then he smiles and looks up.

"The first thing I noticed about you is you have more letters after your name than in it."

He laughs, obviously amused with himself. I give a polite chuckle that's just enough to keep the conversation moving.

He sets the résumé down, folds his hands.

"I'm serious. That tells me you're built for this. Hungry. Smart. Willing to play the long game. That's who we look for. People with vision. We want people who've seen the system's cracks and know how to build on them. So tell me—honestly—is that you?"

I hold his gaze, steady. But something shifts inside me. A small twitch in my stomach.

"I know this world," I say. "Not just from the outside. I know the inside of it. The cracks. The theater. The moments that get cut from the brochure."

He watches me.

"I've seen what happens when the program becomes the product. I've seen kids fall apart in places meant to fix them. I've seen good intentions weaponized. But I've also seen what really works. What actually helps."

He nods slightly. Not in agreement, just that he's heard me.

"Most people who say that," he says, "want to burn it all down. Tear it out by the roots."

"I'm not most people," I say.

There's a pause. He weighs the moment. Then he leans back, changing his tone.

"You know what this place is. You've read the articles, seen the photos, the awards, the retreats with private chefs and custom yoga. People call us luxury recovery. But we're not selling lifestyle. We're selling relief."

He taps the desk lightly.

"When someone's child is unraveling, they'll pay anything for relief. That's the truth most people can't stomach. But you? You get it. I can see that."

I nod once and let the silence stretch out to give me a chance to think about my answer.

"Understanding the game and playing it aren't the same thing."

He smiles without blinking.

"Not yet. Corey, you either learn to play or you get left behind. But I'm betting you're not here to be left behind."

He stands and walks to the glass wall overlooking the property. The view is million dollar: green lawns, infinity pools, a private path winding around a koi pond. It's stunning but just too perfect.

"Let's be honest," he says. "We didn't build this for the average kid. Our clients are diplomats' daughters, hedge fund sons, and celebrities. These families don't just want help. They want a story. A redemption arc with a concierge."

He turns back to me.

"If you want justice, you'll be miserable here. But if you want impact, I'll find you a seat at the table."

I don't answer right away. The truth is, I don't know what I want anymore.

I've carried my own story for so long. It's always been about survival, about proving them wrong. But what happens if I actually get there? What if I cross the line between change and selling out? Maybe those two are closer than I'm willing to admit. Only one way to find out.

"I'm in," I say.

Fields walks back to his desk and shakes my hand again.

"We'll start next week. You'll sit in on programs and shadow leads. You've got something we can use here. Don't waste it."

I nod and smile as I stand.

"Looking forward to it."

And I am, but that makes me feel uneasy.

The sun is sharp. I slide on my sunglasses and cross the stone walkway toward the sports car they rented for me. The building behind me gleams. It's all about money and second chances here. Perfect and safe from the outside.

The car is low and quiet when I start it. Every detail is smooth, expensive, and effortless.

I sit still for a moment before pulling out. The seat fits around me in a way that feels strangely comforting. Like something designed to make you feel important. And it works. For a second, I lean into it. The ease. The quiet.

I look down at my hands on the wheel. Clean nails. Steady. I look like I'm in control. But I don't feel that way. Not entirely.

Because this job, this place, this version of me fit perfectly into the kind of world that almost broke me as a kid. And now I've walked back in, dressed like I belong, speaking the language fluently. Smiling in the right places. Laughing when required.

I told myself I was here to fix the system. But sitting here, in this car, in this suit—I'm not sure if I came to change the system or to finally be accepted by it.

And maybe that's the biggest risk of all.

The engine hums quietly. I don't move.

I just sit there, letting the weight of it settle. I like how it feels to be seen as someone with value. Someone who matters.

And that might be the most dangerous thing of all.